WHO SAYS YOU CAN'T TEACH SCIENCE?

Good Year Books

are available for preschool through grade 12 and for every basic curriculum subject plus many enrichment areas. For more Good Year Books, contact your local bookseller or educational dealer. For a complete catalog with information about other Good Year Books, please write:

Good Year Books
An imprint of Pearson Learning
299 Jefferson Road
Parsippany, New Jersey 07054-0480
1-800-321-3106
www.pearsonlearning.com

WHO SAYS YOU CAN'T TEACH SCIENCE?

Alan Ticotsky
Carlisle Public Schools
Carlisle, Massachusetts

Good Year Books
Parsippany, New Jersey

To Jane
who has helped make this
and many other dreams come true.

For helpful revision suggestions
the author and publisher are grateful to
Alison Beskin, Anne Cernak, and Loretta Wilson.

ISBN 0-673-18107-3

17 18-EBI-99 98

CONTENTS

INTRODUCTION

Who Says You Can't Teach Science? is designed to help adults guide children toward an understanding of the natural world. It presents a step-by-step experiential introduction to general science developed over many years of teaching in an elementary school classroom.

Teachers can use these hands-on activities with children from kindergarten through grade six. Parents, camp counselors, and youth group leaders should also find this book useful. Studying science is important and exciting and should be a part of every primary student's education. Teachers in the early grades often face restrictions—such as lack of aptitude, time, money, and space—that seem to preclude teaching science. But this book will show you that you *can* teach science.

Overcoming Lack of Aptitude

Although many teachers are intimidated by teaching science, you probably know much more about science than you think, and you certainly know a great deal more than the children you teach. To build upon the knowledge you already possess, spend an hour or two browsing through science books designed for children (in the 500's at your school or local library); they will educate you quickly. If you are still feeling insecure, each chapter in *Who Says You Can't Teach Science?* contains enough background information to enable you to teach the scientific principles involved.

Overcoming Lack of Time

Reading, math, writing, spelling, grammar . . . the subjects that are higher than science on a teacher's priority list can go on and on. In many cases, science has to be "snuck in." But you can find opportunities for brief science lessons. Try to schedule a specific period for science each week; then stick with it. And be alert for short stretches of time; they are especially useful for follow-up discussions.

Science can be integrated successfully with other academic subjects. For example, maintaining a science notebook also can improve penmanship. Writing up the results of an experiment augments the language arts curriculum, and measurement skills get reinforced in many science activities and applications. Students who consider the effect of science upon society are sharpening social studies skills, and, of course, reading a supplementary science book pays dividends in improved reading as well as in greater awareness of scientific knowledge.

Many teachers reserve some "free time," usually at the end of the day. Guide students to the classroom science center or science table during their free time. Insofar as your own free time is concerned, *Who Says You Can't Teach Science?* has been designed to keep planning time to a minimum. A list of required materials appears at the beginning of each activity, and the instructions for each experiment are easy to read and follow without elaborate preparation.

Overcoming Lack of Space

All you need for a science center is a fairly large, flat space—preferably near a sink—where things won't be frequently disturbed. Even a shelf or counter top can be an effective display and storage area. Most of the activities in this book can be done at the children's desks or work tables, or even outdoors where nearly any terrain will be suitable and interesting.

Overcoming Lack of Money

None of the activities in *Who Says You Can't Teach Science?* requires expensive equipment. For the most part, they involve everyday items that not only ensure economy in the classroom but also enable children to repeat or continue the activities at home. In addition, children enjoy grouping together for science, making it unnecessary for each one to have individual materials.

Although a list of inexpensive items for a science center appears at the end of this introduction, check with other teachers and with your students before you buy anything. School closets often contain dusty but otherwise perfect science materials, and the children can provide an ample supply of items from the "things to accumulate" list.

You *Can* Teach Science!

Now that you know that you can teach science, here are some reasons why you would want to teach it. Science in the primary grades fosters discovery and appreciation. It also helps students learn to think and to see the world in a logical manner. You do a great service for a child when you help instill a sense of wonder and curiosity about the world, as opposed to merely repeating facts available elsewhere. Therefore, teaching the scientific method—that is, forming a hypothesis and testing it—is far more important than having students memorize names and statistics.

Some children who respond negatively to "schoolwork" enjoy and excel in science. They may struggle with academic tasks but work well with their hands, deriving new pride from this mastery. These activities do not ask children (or teachers) to duplicate preconceived results. They are designed so that children can make observations and reach their own conclusions.

The three sections of *Who Says You Can't Teach Science?* help you lead your students through a general introduction to science. The first section deals with the materials of the Earth: air (a gas), water (a liquid), and dirt and rocks (solids). It concludes with a look at the Earth as a whole, as a sphere in space. The second section explores certain principles: motion, sound, light and color, simple machines, and magnetism and electricity. The final section looks at plant and animal life, including the human body. Of course, you can determine your selection of activities on the basis of student interest, availability of materials or resource people, field trips, and other relevant variables.

As you make your way through these three sections, students are bound to gain an appreciation of their planet and the need for strategies to protect its resources and inhabitants. In addition, class morale and individual self-esteem are bound to grow as children get involved in and excited about science activities. *Who Says You Can't Teach Science?* can help you make science meaningful and enjoyable in the elementary school classroom.

Setting Up A Classroom Science Center

Basic Beginning Equipment
    magnifying lenses
    directional compasses
    metric and English measuring tools
    magnets (be sure to keep magnets away from the compasses!)
    mirrors
    thermometers
    simple pulley
    garden trowels

Handy Items To Accumulate (ask for student donations)
    newspaper to cover tables
    nature magazines
    glass jars with tops
    flower pots
    planting trays
    sturdy boxes and containers—especially shoe boxes, oatmeal containers, and plastic food containers with snap-on lids.

PART 1
What Is The World Made Of?

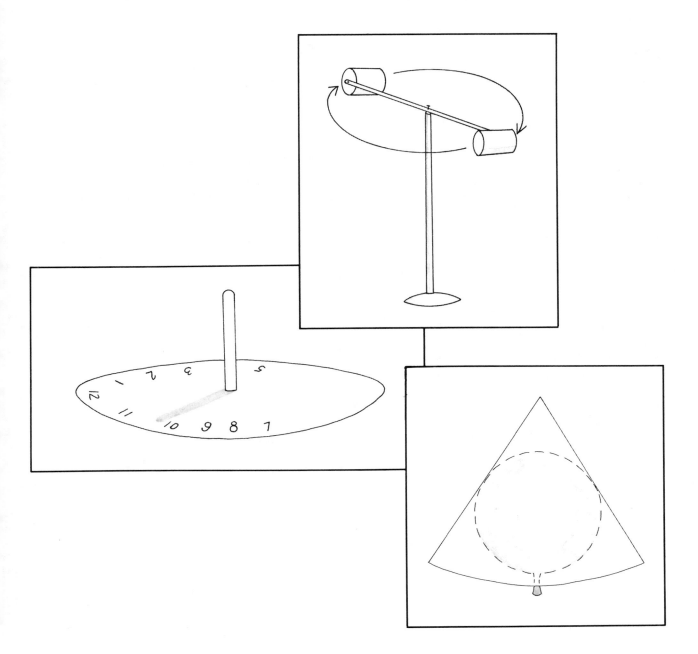

 **AIR**

If you ask children what is all around them, they will first mention all the solid objects they see. When pressed further, many will answer, "Nothing."

That is why the first concept they must discover is that air is all around us and takes up space. There are many experiments and demonstrations that illustrate this concept. Here are a few to get you started.

AIR TAKES UP SPACE

Materials and Supplies
cup (preferably transparent)
crumpled paper
sink or container full of water

Stuff the crumpled paper firmly into the cup so that it does not fall out when the cup is inverted. Now push the cup into the water, open side down. Pull the cup out and ask students to see if the paper got wet. The paper stays dry because air takes up space and creates a barrier between the paper and the water.

Immerse the cup again, but this time tip it so that air bubbles escape. The soaked paper shows what happens when no air is present to serve as a barrier between the crumpled paper and the water.

AIR CAN SLOW DOWN FALLING OBJECTS

Materials and Supplies
rocks and other objects of different weights
scrap paper
paper clips

First, demonstrate Galileo's discovery that two objects of different weights will fall at equal speeds. Be sure to drop many objects of different weights, but avoid objects light enough to encounter significant air resistance. Standing on a chair or table will enhance the experiment by increasing the distance that the objects fall.

Once you convince the skeptics that objects fall at equal speeds, repeat the experiment with a ball of crumpled paper and a flat sheet of paper dropped simultaneously. The flat sheet, of course, encounters greater air resistance, falling more slowly as it makes irregular swoops.

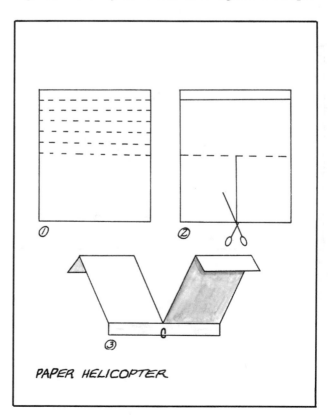

PAPER HELICOPTER

The discovery of air resistance is sure to spark interest in designing parachutes, airplanes, helicopters, and so forth. You can organize a contest to see who can create the parachute that stays aloft longest after being dropped from an established release point.

Discuss how seeds ride through the air, and have the children look for examples. Then have them make the paper helicopters as illustrated, which imitate the motion of maple seeds.

A FLAME NEEDS AIR

> *Materials and Supplies*
> candle
> set of glass containers of different sizes
> matches

Light the candle, and then—one at a time—place each of the glass containers over it. Measure how long the flame continued to burn under each container.

The children will discover that oxygen, a component of air, is needed for combustion. Once the oxygen is exhausted, the candle flame goes out. Since the larger containers contain more oxygen, the flame lasts longer in them than in the smaller containers.

AIR HAS WEIGHT

> *Materials and Supplies*
> balloons
> yard or meter stick
> string
> pin

Tie a balloon to each end of the stick. Hang the stick on a string (or balance it on your finger) so that the stick is parallel to the ground.

Explain to the children how balancing shows that equal weight exists on both halves of the stick.

Now pop one balloon. The resulting imbalance is really a comparison of the weight of an inflated balloon with that of a deflated one. The one that is still inflated is heavier, proving that air has weight.

Another interesting set of experiments explores the way air performs work.

AIR DOES WORK: 1

> *Materials and Supplies*
> drinking straws
> marbles or ping-pong balls

Children enjoy moving objects by directing a flow of air at them. You can even organize races in which the children blow through straws to propel marbles or ping-pong balls over a designated course.

AIR DOES WORK: 2

> *Materials and Supplies*
> drinking straws
> scrap paper

Drawing in on a straw creates a vacuum, a concept children are familiar with from the household vacuum cleaner. Let the children use the straw's vacuum to pick up scraps of paper.

Next, demonstrate how they can stop sucking but still preserve the vacuum by placing a finger over the end of the straw.

Finally, hold two strips of paper at the end of the straw and try directing air between them. Rather than being blown apart, the strips are pulled together by the vacuum created as the air moves past the paper.

AIR DOES WORK: 3

> *Materials and Supplies*
> balloons
> books or other flat and heavy objects

Place an uninflated balloon under a book. Have the children watch the book rise as you blow up the balloon. Then see how many books a single balloon can lift. Children can work in groups to lift a heavy object with several balloons.

Have the children list other ways that air does work—e.g., blowing up automobile and bicycle tires, inflatable boats.

Air moves and changes. Here are three examples of moving air experiments, but don't overlook such common observations as smoke drifting from a chimney or dust moving in a beam of sunlight streaming through a window.

HOT AIR RISES: 1

> *Materials and Supplies*
> small flags
> (tissue paper or light fabric on sticks or pencils)

Try to locate air currents in your classroom with homemade flags—paper or fabric taped to sticks. Upward currents should occur near heaters; downward currents can be found near drafty spots. Have the children put together a map or diagram of "wind conditions" inside the classroom.

When you finish the experiment, you might want to plug up the drafty areas with weatherstripping. Not only will your classroom be more comfortable in winter but also your students will appreciate the "real life" applications of scientific principles.

HOT AIR RISES: 2

> *Materials and Supplies*
> balloon
> soda bottle

If your room has forced air heat, stretch the balloon over the neck of the bottle and place the bottle over a heating register. The air in bottle will rise as it gets warmer, eventually causing the balloon to become partially inflated. Hint: It helps to inflate and deflate the balloon several times before doing the experiment so that it expands more easily as the warm air enters it.

If your room has radiators, attach an inflated balloon to a string and hang the balloon near one of the radiators. Have the children note any movements of the balloon in reaction to the air currents created by the hot radiator.

WIND IS MOVING AIR

> *Materials and Supplies*
> flag or pennant
> directional compass

Place a flag or pennant outside, and draw compass directions for north, south, east, and west around its base. You now have a wind direction indicator for your class.

Have the children record wind direction information—e.g., from which direction is the prevailing wind?—on a graph or calendar. Then see if they can generalize about weather patterns. Does a particular wind direction indicate fair weather while another direction means inclement conditions?

Your class can record other weather information in addition to wind direction. Temperature, humidity, air pressure, and wind velocity are all fairly easy to monitor without costly equipment.

A WEATHER STATION

Materials and Supplies
two bottles; one wide mouthed,
the other long necked
two paper cups
wooden dowel with a hole through it
weather thermometers
piece of cloth
paper

Your class, no matter what the grade level, can construct a simple weather station. Start with a barometer for measuring air pressure. Take the wide-mouthed bottle and fill it about half full with water. Turn the long-necked bottle upside down and put it into the wide-mouthed one. Fasten a graduated scale (a piece of paper marked in even intervals) to the back of the neck of the inverted bottle. Make certain that you and the children can read the scale through the neck of the wide-mouthed bottle.

As the weather changes, the water will move up and down. Higher air pressure pushes down on the water in the wide-mouthed bottle, forcing it up into the neck of the inverted bottle. As the air pressure drops, the water returns to the lower bottle.

BAROMETER

To create a gauge for measuring wind velocity, mount paper cups at opposite ends of a balanced dowel. By counting the revolutions of the dowel over an established period of time, children can estimate wind speed. The wind direction indicator described in "WIND IS MOVING AIR" can also provide information on wind velocity. The relative stiffness of the flag shows whether wind speed is strong or weak.

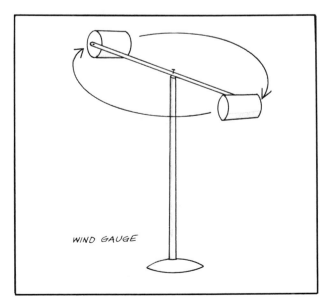

WIND GAUGE

To measure relative humidity (the percentage of water vapor in the air), compare the temperature reading of a dry thermometer with one whose bulb is wrapped in a damp cloth. The greater the difference in temperature, the drier the air is.

Be sure to measure and record the temperature at the same time every day. And remember that the thermometer must be placed out of the sun. If possible, try to have a thermometer with both Celsius and Fahrenheit scales.

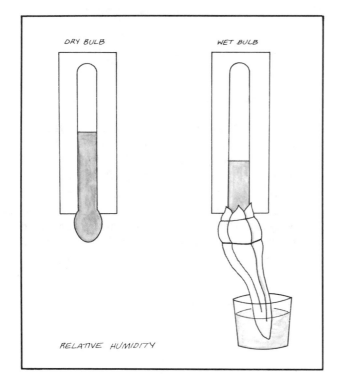

RELATIVE HUMIDITY

WIND CAN PRODUCE ENERGY

Materials and Supplies
scissors
paper
tape
pencil
drinking straw

Children enjoy designing their own wind-powered ships and planes, and here is a project which should elicit some creative thinking.

Organize a paper airplane contest or clinic. Kids can teach each other as they build sailboats and gliders. Ask the children to practice building wind-powered spinners or pinwheels. You can ask for suggestions about design or plunge ahead with a group "think tank."

Start the demonstration of wind-powered spinners by showing how a piece of paper can be rolled into a cone. What shape should the "wind catchers" or sails of the spinner be? Support the spinner on a pencil or stick, and make it turn by directing a stream of air at it through a drinking straw. Then see if the wind will make the spinner turn.

Building a simple spinner reinforces the idea that moving air (wind) can do work. You can discuss how wind produces energy by explaining the principle behind a windmill and a turbine. A turbine is an engine turned by a stream of gas or liquid. As the turbine spins it turns a shaft which can produce electricity or supply the power to make machines work.

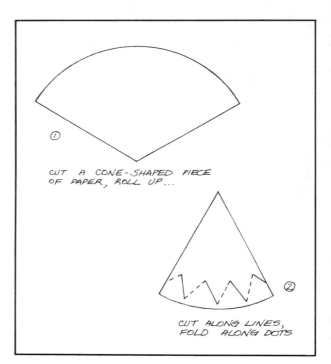

CUT A CONE-SHAPED PIECE OF PAPER, ROLL UP...

CUT ALONG LINES, FOLD ALONG DOTS

WATER

If you have access to a sink and some plastic tubs or trays, you can easily demonstrate many useful lessons about the properties of water.

WHAT FLOATS AND WHAT SINKS?

Materials and Supplies
water
jar with top
sink or large container
metal baking pan
variety of common objects—
e.g., paper clips, eraser, pencil, nails
pebbles or sand
salt

Fill a sink or large container with water. Have the students put everyday items in the water to see whether the items sink or float. Record what happens to each item, and then ask the children to draw general rules about flotation. Be sure to have a metal item that floats—like a baking pan—so that the children will have to consider factors other than the material of which the object is made.

Move on to discuss the Archimedes Principle. Archimedes discovered that displacement, the amount of water pushed aside by an object, is the determining factor in flotation. If the weight of an object is equal to the weight of the fluid displaced, the object will float. It is the Archimedes Principle which explains why steel ships weighing thousands of tons and carrying huge cargoes can float. Because they displace so much water, the ships are held up by the upthrust of the water they displace. The density (weight per unit of volume) of a ship is less than solid steel because the air in the ship is part of its volume.

Partially fill a transparent jar with sand or pebbles and place it in the water-filled sink. Observe how much of the jar is submerged. Now add more sand or pebbles and have the students record what happens to the waterline (it rises). Finally, add salt to the water, stir it until it dissolves, and then ask the children to note whether the jar floats differently in salt water.

THINGS WEIGH LESS IN WATER

Materials and Supplies
container of water
rubber band
string
rock

Loop the string through the rubber band, tie it to the rock, and pick up the rock by lifting the rubber band. Measure the length that the rubber band stretches to as it lifts the rock.

Now place the rock in water and lift it once again. This time the rubber band will not stretch as much as it did before. Repeat the experiment with other objects to show that they all weigh less in water.

Archimedes proved that the weight of an object in water is reduced by the weight of the water that the object displaces. It is, therefore, due to the upthrust of the water that the rock becomes easier to lift in water than from a dry surface.

SOME THINGS DISSOLVE IN WATER

Materials and Supplies
water
sturdy transparent cups
spoons
salt
sugar
sand
baking powder
baking soda
flour
other common substances

Have the children stir the various solids into water in the sturdy transparent cups. Remind them to pause occasionally to allow for settling, and make it a rule that they must stop adding a substance if they cannot clear the bottom by stirring. Emphasize that they should not dispose of any mud or dough down the drain. If you have a source of hot water available, repeat the experiment with warm water and have the children note whether larger amounts of solids can be dissolved.

When you finish the experiment, put each of the mixes on a window sill to evaporate. The solid material will often change to larger crystals after being dissolved.

WATER HAS SURFACE TENSION

Materials and Supplies
water
glass jar with top
pennies or paper clips
string
hammer and nail

Fill a glass nearly to the brim with water. Then gently drop in pennies or paper clips. Students should watch carefully as the water level approaches the top and gradually builds up over the edge. The water surface becomes convex, but surface tension prevents droplets from escaping over the edge.

You can demonstrate the principle of surface tension in other interesting ways. For example, tie a string to a water faucet and extend the string toward a corner of the sink. When you turn on the water, it will flow along the string as if it were iron attracted by a magnet.

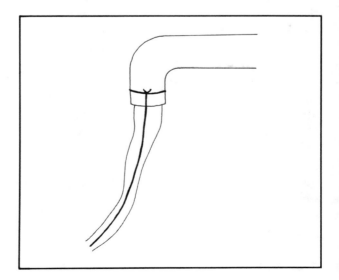

Or, fill a jar with water until it is three-quarters full. Perforate the jar's lid several times with a small nail, screw on the lid, and invert the jar over a sink. When the children ask why the water does not rush out through the holes in the lid, explain that surface tension keeps it from breaking into droplets small enough to escape through the holes.

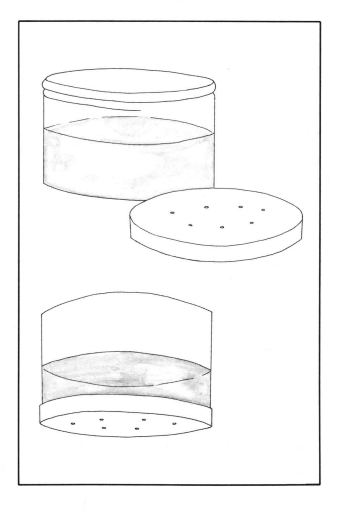

SURFACE TENSION CAN BE BROKEN

Materials and Supplies
sink or a large open container
sturdy paper
scissors
soap (liquid or powder)
water
glass jar with top
oil

Have the children draw and cut out flat paper boats with a notch in the stern. Place the boats on top of the water in the sink or large container. As the boats float around, drop soap or oil into the water at the notch of each boat. The boats will scoot ahead as the soap or oil breaks the surface tension of the water.

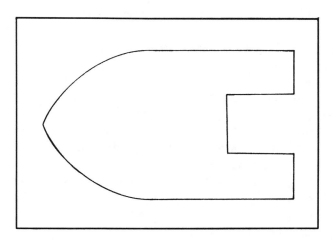

You can use these same materials for another demonstration. Combine water and oil in a glass jar with a top. Ask the children to shake the jar to try to get the liquids to mix. After everyone watches the water and oil separate a few times, add some soap. Now have the children shake the jar once again. The soap will break the surface tension of the water and allow it to surround the oil. The children should be able to draw some conclusions as to why soap is an effective cleaning agent.

WAVES ARE MOTION THROUGH A MEDIUM

Materials and Supplies
rope
ribbon
large container or water table
cork

Choose two children to hold the ends of the rope. One should hold an end steady while the other moves his or her end up and down. Have the rest of the class try to draw a diagram of the rope's movement. Tying a ribbon to the rope can help the children see what happens at a particular point along the length of rope.

This demonstration shows how waves are motion through a medium. A given point moves up and down rather than along the length of the rope, and the rope itself does not travel anywhere.

You can demonstrate that waves pass through water in a similar manner. Create gentle waves in the water table or container, preferably located in a sunny spot so that the children can observe the shadows that the waves create on the bottom of the basin. The patterns are fascinating when waves begin to bounce against walls and reverse direction. A cork or other floater placed on the water will serve the same purpose as the ribbon did on the rope—i.e., focus attention on the wave motion at a particular point.

WATER BENDS LIGHT

Materials and Supplies
water
paper
spoon
glass container
lens or other piece of glass

You can demonstrate how water can act as a magnifying lens. Have the children print a message in tiny letters. Then place a drop of water over part of the message. The water will enlarge the printing by bending the light as a magnifying lens does.

Next, place a spoon in a partially filled glass of water. Ask the children why the spoon appears to be bent or broken. It is, of course, the light and not the spoon that the water is bending.

You can even make your own classroom rainbows. Place drops of water on a window (or on a lens or piece of glass) that receives direct sunlight. You will have to experiment with the angle of the glass to the sun, but the point is that you can duplicate precisely how rainbows are formed—sun shining through water drops.

STUDYING THE WATER CYCLE

Materials and Supplies
two jars (one with a lid)
markers or crayons
mural paper
terrarium materials—glass bowl or empty
fish tank, pebbles, charcoal, potting soil

Where does steam go when water boils? Where does dew come from? Why do drops of water appear on the outside of a glass that contains cold liquid?

Most children are familiar with steam, dew, and condensation, but they may not realize that all three are forms of water. Here is an experiment that children can do to follow the changes from one form of water to another.

Pour some water into two jars, filling both to the same level. Mark that level with tape. Screw the lid tightly onto one jar, but leave the other jar open. Set both jars in the sun for several hours. As the water level drops in the open jar, ask the children to consider where the water has gone.

The "steamed-up" sealed jar should provide an important clue. Place the sealed jar in a cool spot, and—after the jar becomes clear of "fog" once again—ask the children what has happened. They should understand that one form of water is vapor, or gas, and that the vapor condenses back into a liquid when it cools.

As you discuss the water cycle with the children, they should grasp how heat makes water evaporate into the air and how cooling brings it back as condensation. On a greater scale, the sun turns water into vapor which then rises into the atmosphere. As the water cools, it forms clouds and eventually returns to the ground as rain or snow.

Building a terrarium provides a child with his or her own miniature water cycle. Sunlight causes water to evaporate, and the terrarium cover traps it. When the terrarium cools, the water condenses and returns in the form of drops rolling down the interior sides.

You can find many books about plants and gardening that include specific and detailed directions for setting up a terrarium. Simply stated, start with a layer of rocks or pebbles for drainage, add some planting charcoal for filtering odors, and then pour in soil. Add the plants and water well. If there seems to be too much water in the container, leave the top off for a while to allow vapor to escape.

Encourage the children to draw pictures of the water cycle process. While they are drawing, ask the following kinds of questions:

Does all water end up in the sea or in lakes?
No, some water soaks into the ground and is trapped while other water evaporates.

Why are the oceans salty?
Oceans are the lowest points on this planet, and they have received mineral run-off from land for millions of years.

Is water in the ocean lost forever as far as people drinking it is concerned?
No, the sun evaporates ocean water which then can come back down as fresh water in future precipitation.

You can extend a lesson about the water cycle into a discussion about the importance of conservation. The water cycle shows how nature is a closed system which humans must fit or risk upsetting the natural balance. Children should learn to appreciate the necessity for understanding nature rather than trying to control it.

DIRT AND ROCKS

While studying the solid, nonliving parts of our planet, children can practice measuring, categorizing, and observing—all important skills to master.

COLLECTING ROCKS FOR STUDY

> *Materials and Supplies*
> rocks from schoolyard

Begin by having the children collect specimens from the schoolyard. Once the samples are in the classroom, the children should sort them by size and weight. They can also categorize the rocks by hardness, developing a scale of relative hardness by scratching rocks together and learning which ones are not marked by others.

Children may offer to bring sample rocks or whole collections from home to share. While they should be encouraged to do so, it is best to start with the rocks in the schoolyard; a dazzling, eclectic collection might tend to make the schoolyard rocks appear dull by comparison.

You can make your science table a treasure-trove of rock-related items. Put out books that identify rocks as well as books about dinosaurs and other extinct creatures whose remains are frozen in rocks—fossils. Set out magnifying tools so that the children can examine the specimens they bring in from the schoolyard and other places.

ROCKS CAN BE BROKEN

> *Materials and Supplies*
> coffee can with lid
> variety of rock specimens
> pieces of brick or cement
> water

This experiment allows children to break bricks and soft stones. Place some pieces of brick and the stones into a coffee can with some water. After placing the lid securely on the can, have the children shake the can a specific number of times. Then open the can and have everyone observe how broken the stones have become. Repeat the experiment without water in the can to show how soft rocks break up more quickly when wet (due to the dissolving power of water) than when dry.

Hint: This is a very noisy experiment and should be done outdoors or when you are sure that other classes won't be disturbed.

It will also become clear that bricks break up soft rocks (try to use thin, flat specimens) while hard rocks tend to break up the bricks. Explain to the children—using pictures if possible—that many of the beautiful rock formations of the American Southwest and those found along shorelines are the result of softer rocks being worn away, leaving harder rocks behind.

Encourage the children to look closely at their broken up rocks. They should try to guess if a rock is igneous (from the root word "ignite"—rocks that have formed by cooling from a molten state) or sedimentary. Sedimentary rocks are those produced by compressed layers of rock fragments. Careful examination can often reveal a crystallized structure (igneous) or stratified layers (sedimentary). You can also mention a third major type of rock: metamorphic. Metamorphic rocks, which are those that have been transformed in shape by pressure and heat, can be either igneous or sedimentary in origin.

Ask each child to speculate on the history of his or her favorite rock and perhaps write a story about its "life." If you teach in the northern section of the continent, remember to discuss the glaciers which carried rocks hundreds of miles as they spread over the land during the ice ages.

CRYSTALS FORM WHEN SOME THINGS COOL

Materials and Supplies
salt
string
pencil or stick
water
cup or glass
magnifying lens or microscope

Let the children examine salt through a magnifying lens or microscope. Point out the beauty and symmetry of each salt crystal's structure, and the advantages of a magnified view compared to the naked eye's perspective.

Next, dissolve some salt in water by stirring the mixture in a cup. Suspend a string into the water from a pencil or stick laid across the cup. If the string tends to float, tie a nail or paper clip to the end. Leave the cup on a window sill for several days and check each day as more water evaporates. Have the children watch for crystals to form; then let them view the crystals through a magnifying lens or microscope once again. They should note that the individual salt cubes have changed into larger crystal units.

MAKING A CRYSTAL GARDEN

Materials and Supplies
base: piece of brick, sponge,
or charcoal or coal
water
bluing (found with bleaches and
detergents in supermarkets)
ammonia
salt
food coloring

Wet the piece of brick and place it in a shallow dish. Combine equal amounts of water, bluing, and ammonia, and pour the mixture over the brick. Sprinkle with salt and add some food coloring to brighten up the garden.

Crystals should form overnight. Add water and ammonia every few days to encourage crystal growth.

Children should understand that many of the rocks they find and study—as well as the beautiful rock structures they see in pictures—were formed by the process of crystallization.

SOIL CONSISTS OF BROKEN ROCKS AND ORGANIC MATERIAL

Materials and Supplies
several identical containers (cans or jars)
dirt samples
scale or balance
package of fast-sprouting seeds

Children learn about the composition of dirt by collecting and comparing different types of soil. Encourage them to gather as many distinct samples as possible from the garden, lawn, playground, roadside, and woods. Ask each child to bring in at least one container of dirt.

Put equal volumes of each soil sample in the containers. Weigh them and record the data. Let the children speculate as to why some types of dirt are heavier than others. Ask them how the following soil components could affect weight: rocks, organic material, moisture. Spread out some of each sample so that students can examine its composition.

Next, add a measured amount of water to each soil sample in the containers. Water will immediately soak into some soils while pooling on top of others. Which sample can accept the most water before overflowing?

If earthworms are present in the soil, the water will drive them up toward the surface. These fascinating creatures deserve some study and can add an extra science lesson to your demonstration.

Discuss which soil sample has the most organic material (humus). Although decaying plant and animal material often contributes greatly to soil fertility and thereby benefits gardens, the presence of humus does not by itself determine fertility. Soil from pine woods, for example, contains a great deal of organic material, but it is so acidic that many plants will not thrive in it.

Have the children plant some fast-sprouting seeds in each of the various soil samples. They will then quickly discover which soil is the most suitable for that type of plant.

EROSION IS THE WASHING AWAY OF SOIL

Materials and Supplies
large tray or box (lined with plastic if not waterproof)
grass seed
watering can or bottle with spout
mound of dirt
water

This entertaining experiment introduces students to the important subject of soil conservation. Start by having the children construct a mountain of dirt in a large tray or box. They can add small stones to simulate boulders and twigs for trees, and they can even build model homes and other structures.

Water the dirt mountain thoroughly and watch while stones, twigs, and structures change position as the ground erodes. Then plant grass seed. Once the grass appears, repeat the heavy watering and see if the grass can retard soil erosion.

Take walks with the children around the schoolyard, noting places where erosion is occurring. Then—after getting permission from the school's maintenance staff—let the children plant in the problem areas in an effort to conserve the schoolyard's soil.

MAKING MODELS OF FOSSILS

Materials and Supplies
plaster of Paris or other molding material
leaves
twigs or other plant pieces
animal bones and feathers

After preparing the plaster mixture, press leaves or other specimens into it to make a clear, detailed impression. Then remove the specimens and let the plaster mixture harden. The children can study their plaster fossils and try to identify the tree or plant from which the specimen was taken.

Emphasize to the children that in the formation of a real fossil, a leaf or other specimen would have been buried in mud. Eventually, a print of the leaf would harden into stone.

Fossils are found in formations of sedimentary rather than igneous rock. In moist sediment, plant and animal remains decay slowly enough for a natural cast to be formed around them. Millions of years after the living organism was buried, we can study just what it looked like through its fossil remains.

HOW MOUNTAINS ARE FORMED

Materials and Supplies
clay

Children can learn a great deal about topography from working with clay models of the Earth. After they form clay into spheres, encourage them to squeeze and twist, steadily and gently, applying pressure to form mountain ranges on their miniature planets. This is a fun and productive lesson designed to stimulate thinking about prehistoric eras when much of our present topography came into being through the shifting and sliding of rocks. The pressures they exert with their hands on the clay are comparable to the dynamic forces which caused mountains to rise during geologically more active times.

You can even use the clay spheres to demonstrate plate tectonics—the widely held theory that Earth's outer crust consists of huge chunks of "shell" sliding about. According to this theory, the points at which these chunks contact one another are likely to be areas of extensive earthquake and volcanic activity. After the children sculpt "continents" and slide them around their clay globes, have them examine a real globe carefully. Ask if they can see how the land masses might be rearranged like the pieces of a puzzle to fit neatly together into one supercontinent.

EARTH IN SPACE

After studying the components of the Earth—air, water, dirt and rocks—children will be able to visualize the planet as a sphere in space. They should then try to understand the concept of the Earth as a spaceship upon which we all ride. For example, they should try to imagine themselves viewing the Earth from beyond our atmosphere. If they can see this planet as a finite sphere in space, they can begin to appreciate the crucial difference between renewable and nonrenewable resources. In this context, the water cycle appears as an elegantly simple system which people need to respect and not disrupt.

To set the stage for a global perspective, fill the classroom science area with books and pictures about space, a globe, an atlas, and other materials relating to the oceans, continents, and atmosphere. You may even want to cover a unit usually done as part of social studies: the European explorations and discoveries during the fifteenth and sixteenth centuries.

COMPARING THE DISTANCES BETWEEN PLANETS

Materials and Supplies
meter or yardstick

Children enjoy arranging themselves into a model of the solar system that gives them a feeling for the distances involved. Here is a scale that reduces the solar system—mind-boggling even to an adult—to about the size of a football field.

Choose a point to represent the sun at one end of a football, soccer, or other open field. Measure 80 centimeters (.8 meter) from this point, and place a child there to represent Mercury, the planet closest to the sun. It is better to measure in meters rather than yards for this activity because the metric system permits distances to be expressed as decimals or multiples of the same unit, the meter. On the other hand, since a football field is already marked off in yards, you might find it more convenient to estimate tenths of yards or to measure each tenth as 3.6 inches.

Continuing on with your solar system, place the child representing Venus at 1.4 meters from the sun. "Earth" should stand two meters from the sun while "Mars" should be positioned at three meters from the sun.

Now the distances between planets and between planets and the sun increase dramatically. Use the following chart to position your "planets" properly.

Planet	Distance from Sun
Mercury	0.8 meter or yard
Venus	1.4 meters or yards
Earth	2.0 meters or yards
Mars	3.0 meters or yards
Jupiter	10.4 meters or yards
Saturn	19.0 meters or yards
Uranus	38.4 meters or yards
Neptune	60.0 meters or yards
Pluto	79.0 meters or yards

Remember to emphasize that the sun is in the center of the solar system. The planets, therefore, usually are not strung out in a straight line. Of course, if you have access to a large field, you can place the "sun" in the middle of the field and measure the distances out to the planets in a number of different directions.

One interesting fact that you might want to mention is that the orbits of the two most distant planets—Neptune and Pluto—cross. As a matter of fact, until the year 1999, Neptune will be farther from the sun than Pluto.

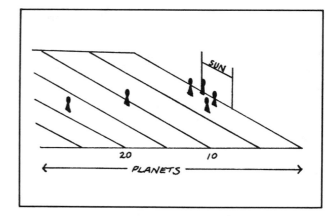

COMPARING THE SIZES OF THE PLANETS

Materials and Supplies
paper
scissors
ruler
circle-drawing compass

Draw and then cut out a paper disk measuring one inch in diameter. This disk will represent Earth. Now prepare similar disks to represent the other planets. Use the chart below as a guide to the relative sizes of the planets.

Planet	Disk Diameter in Inches
Mercury	0.4
Venus	0.9
Mars	0.5
Jupiter	11.2
Saturn	9.4
Uranus	3.7
Neptune	3.8
Pluto	0.5

If you are committed to using metric measurement, you can start with a disk of ten centimeters in diameter to represent Earth. Diameters for the other disks would then be as follows:

Planet	Disk Diameter in Centimeters
Mercury	4
Venus	9
Mars	5
Jupiter	112
Saturn	94
Uranus	37
Neptune	38
Pluto	5

If you want to add the sun to this demonstration, you will need a disk with a diameter of 110 inches or, if you are using the metric scale, eleven meters. You might consider drawing the sun with chalk on the playground rather than making a paper disk.

COMPARING BOTH THE DISTANCE AND SIZE OF PLANETS

Materials and Supplies
measuring wheel or stick
metric scale showing millimeters
small rocks
sand

To show both the size of the entire solar system and the distances between the planets in one scale model is difficult because planet size becomes unmanageably small and the distances impractically great. Using the scale below, however, you can represent the size and

distance of the first few planets. Then point out distant landmarks to represent planets farther away. This demonstration can go a long way toward introducing children to the enormity of space.

	Distance from Sun in Meters	Diameter in Millimeters
Sun	0	90.0
Mercury	4	0.3
Venus	4	0.3
Earth	10	0.9
Mars	15	0.5
Jupiter	52	10.0
Saturn	95	8.4
Uranus	192	3.3
Neptune	300	3.4
Pluto	395	0.4

Take the class out to an open field, and use tiny pebbles or grains of sand to represent as many of the planets as you can. You can use a softball to represent the sun.

For example, you can show the relative size and distance of Jupiter by placing a small marble 52 meters away from the softball. But tiny Pluto, the size of a speck of sand (half a millimeter) would have to be farther away than four football fields. To represent Alpha Centauri, a triple star system and our nearest stellar neighbor, would require two softballs and a small marble more than 6,000 kilometers (4,000 miles) away in this scale model.

You can also discuss how distance can be expressed in time. It takes about eight and a half minutes for a ray of light to travel from the sun to the Earth. That same ray requires nearly six hours to reach Pluto. Similarly, light emitted by Alpha Centauri takes more than four years to reach our planet.

USING THE SUN'S ENERGY

All life on Earth depends on the sun. Help the children think of ways in which we depend on the sun to work for us—e.g., dry clothes, grow plants. Explain to your students what fossil fuels are and how they are becoming in short supply. Discuss the environmental problems created when fossil fuels are extracted and burned, and tell the children how more and more people are looking toward the sun as a power source.

Here are some activities that show a few ways in which the sun can help us.

PRINTING SUN PICTURES

Materials and Supplies
colored paper
tape
scissors

Have the students draw and cut out a picture or a lettered message on sturdy paper. Tape the cut-out portion to a piece of strong, colored construction paper. Make sure that the tape is rolled up and hidden between the cut-out and the colored paper.

Leave the work on a sunny window sill or in a protected spot outdoors. The sun will bleach the paper around the shapes or letters so that when the children remove their cut-outs, they will see their drawing or message "printed" by the sun on the construction paper. The longer the paper is left in the sun, the greater will be the contrast between the hidden, shaded area and the exposed, bleached area.

COLLECTING HEAT FROM THE SUN

Materials and Supplies
colored fabric scraps
glass jars
thermometers
empty fish tank or terrarium case

This demonstration shows which colors best collect heat and which best reflect it. Lay scraps of fabric of different colors—but preferably of the same material—on snow in a sunny place. Note which colors promote the most rapid melting. By cutting the fabric into letters or shapes, children can melt messages or pictures into the snow. If you have no access to snow, place a thermometer under each piece of fabric and check temperatures periodically.

To demonstrate the heating potential of solar energy, set an empty fish tank or terrarium in the sun. Let the children heat water in glass jars inside the tank. Use thermometers to measure how high the temperature can get inside the glass enclosure. Then discuss passive solar heating—a concept kids are familiar with from entering a closed car on a sunny day.

TELLING TIME BY THE SUN

Materials and Supplies
post driven into the ground
measuring stick
paper plates
small sticks

Drive a stake into the ground or use an existing post to record data about the length and position of its shadow at specific times throughout the day. Try to use an isolated or protected spot where you can mark out the shadow's position on the ground.

After several observations, children should be able to make sundials of their own, using a paper plate as the dial and a straight stick as the shadow caster.

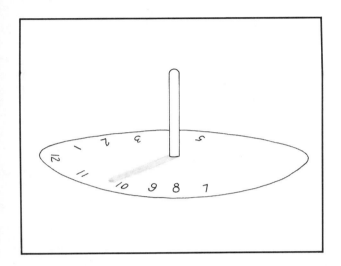

TELLING DIRECTION BY THE SUN

Materials and Supplies
compass
watch (optional)

Take the children outside at regular intervals on a sunny day. Use compasses to determine the direction of the sun. From these observations, the children should write out some generalizations about the direction of the sun at different times of day. For example, the sun is at the southeast early in the day and at the southwest late in the day; at noon it is approximately due south.

You can demonstrate with a globe how the Earth rotates from west to east, which makes the sun appear to move from east to west.

Children with watches can do an interesting experiment. Have them aim the hour hands of

their watches directly at the sun. Then have them bisect, or divide in half, the angle between the hour hand and twelve o'clock. The result will be a line pointing directly south.

BUILDING ROCKET SHIPS

Materials and Supplies
cylindrical oatmeal box
balloons
tape
paper
scissors
drinking straws
string

Designing space ships really captures the interest of children, and using balloons as power sources teaches them how rockets actually work.

First, inflate a balloon and then let the air out of it so that the kids can see how propulsion of air sends the balloon flying in the opposite direction from its lip. Real rockets work on the same propulsion principle—i.e., Newton's third law of motion: for every action there is an equal and opposite reaction.

Next, tape a straw to the outside of an oatmeal box. Run a string through the straw and tie the two ends to two convenient points (e.g., chairs) in order to make a track. Inflate a balloon inside the oatmeal box. When you let go of the balloon, the released air will propel the oatmeal box forward so that it slides along the string.

Outdoors, students can use balloons in a similar manner to propel cone-shaped rockets made from sturdy paper.

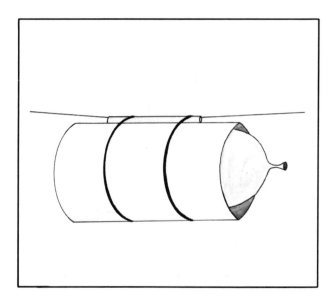

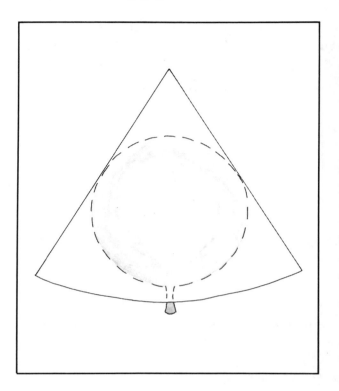

PART 2
How Do Things Work On Earth?

MOTION

While some laws of motion are obvious to children, others seem illogical. Children gain a better understanding of physical properties if they are allowed to discover patterns for themselves. Their measurement skills may not be sufficiently accurate for sophisticated experiments, but children can benefit immensely from early training in record-keeping.

Here are some activities which illustrate natural laws.

THINGS BALANCE ON THEIR CENTERS OF GRAVITY

Materials and Supplies
cork
pin
two forks

Children know that gravity exerts a downward force on things ("down" meaning toward the center of the Earth). This experiment shows how equalizing weight around and below a center of gravity enhances balance.

Poke a pin through a cork. Then stick two forks into opposite ends of the cork. The cork will balance on the pin when the forks hang over the edges of a table.

MAKING A COIN STAND UP

Materials and Supplies
large coin (half dollar or larger)
two forks

This experiment, like the one above, shows how equal weight applied around and below an object lowers its center of gravity.

Attach two forks to a large coin as shown in the drawing below. Position the coin at the edge of a table so that the forks hang down below it. The equal weight of the two forks lowers the coin's center of gravity and permits it to stand on edge.

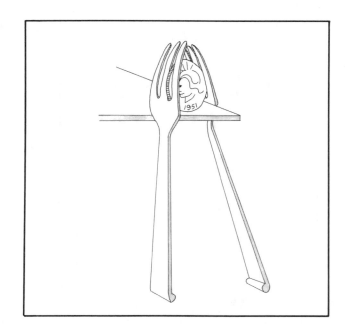

MAKING A BRIDGE OF BOOKS

Materials and Supplies
books

Stack the books near the edge of a table, and let the children see how far off the end of the table they can balance the top book. Then let them see if they can make the books reach out farther by extending the middle book in the pile beyond the others.

The previous activities showed that the center of gravity is the balance point, and children should now be able to deduce what causes the books to fall: When the weight of the books extending beyond the edge of the table becomes too great, the center of gravity is no longer over the table, and the books fall.

Once they understand this natural law, the children can have fun seeing how great a distance they can span by stacking books from two end points, extending the piles toward each other until they meet.

A PENDULUM SWINGS IN STEADY PATTERNS

> *Materials and Supplies*
> uniform weights (any fairly heavy objects that are compact and easy to tie to a string)
> string
> slow-pouring funnel (sturdy paper rolled into a cone with a pin hole at the bottom will do)
> salt or free-flowing sand

Create several pendulums using similar weights and string lengths, and then let the children count the number of times a pendulum swings in a half minute. If the children work in pairs, one holding the string steady and one releasing the weight, there is no need to attach the pendulum to a stand.

Now try varying the weight, the string length, and the angle of the string at the release point. In each case, have the children count the number of times the pendulum swings in a half min-

ute, and let them graph the results (see the example below). This exercise gives children a chance to use scientific method—i.e., the use of variables in a controlled experiment.

Pendulum Graph

Weight	Length of String	Angle of Release	Swings/ Minute
10 grams	50 cm	90°	42
10 grams	50 cm	45°	40
20 grams	50 cm	90°	40
20 grams	50 cm	45°	40
20 grams	25 cm	90°	66
20 grams	25 cm	45°	63
10 grams	25 cm	90°	63
10 grams	25 cm	45°	64
20 grams	100 cm	90°	24
20 grams	100 cm	45°	25
10 grams	100 cm	90°	24
10 grams	100 cm	45°	24

Not only will the children find the data interesting, but they can use the data to generate some rules for pendulum motion. Ask them:

What is the effect of lengthening the string? What happens when you shorten it?
Does the amount of weight on the string affect the number of times the pendulum swings per half minute?
Is the release point a significant factor in pendulum motion?

To create a visually interesting experiment, make a pendulum with a slow-pouring funnel at the end of the string. Fill the funnel with sand or salt, and place a piece of black paper underneath. Have the children note the differences in patterns formed on the paper as you vary the angle of release.

EXPLORING CIRCULAR MOTION

Materials and Supplies
bucket
rope
water or tennis balls

Fill the bucket about half full with water or tennis balls. Tie a rope tightly to the handle, or just hold the handle tightly in your hand. Swing the bucket around in a full circle, and have the children watch what happens to its contents. Explain that the circular motion pushes the water or balls against the bottom of the bucket, preventing them from spilling out.

MAKING A CIRCULAR MOTION MACHINE

Materials and Supplies
large spool or paper towel core
rope or strong string
rock or weight
spoon

To make a neat gadget for the further exploration of circular motion, tie one end of the rope around a rock. Put the other end through the spool or towel core and tie it to the spoon. The rock and spoon should be about the same weight.

Now, while holding the towel core, rotate your wrist so that the spoon begins to circle around the top of the core. Watch the rock rise as the centrifugal force of the spoon lifts the rock. Vary the speed at which the spoon rotates, and have the children note changes in the position of the rock.

OBSERVING MOTION IN TWO DIRECTIONS

Materials and Supplies
rocks or balls

Mark a spot on the ground or place a target on a spot. Have each child hold a rock or ball and run fast toward the spot, dropping the rock—without stopping or slowing down—when they reach the spot. The child dropping the rock should then come back to see where it landed while the other children observe near the target.

Then have each child stand above the target and drop the rock. What should become clear is that an object dropped from a moving start retains some of the original motion. The horizontal component of the rock's motion—that is, its being carried by a running child—should carry it beyond the target. Once they understand the principle, let the children try to hit the target without slowing down.

Another way to demonstrate this principle is to have the children drop a ball from a swing, trying to have it land on a spot beneath them. Well-coordinated students can try holding the ball between their feet while swinging so that they have both hands free for holding on. Others should use a ball small enough that they can hold onto it while keeping two hands on the swing.

OBJECTS CAN CAUSE CHAIN REACTIONS

Materials and Supplies
balls or marbles
dominoes

To introduce the concept of chain reaction motion, set up four balls or marbles so that they touch each other in a straight line. Roll a fifth one into the end of the line, and have the children watch carefully to see what happens. Explain that the force of the fifth ball is transmitted through each ball in the line until the last one rolls away from the group.

Children enjoy setting up intricate chains of dominoes and then keeping track of how long it takes for the chains to fall. In fact, this form of inventive exploration is well suited to independent working. Have them discover whether a domino chain reaction functions at a constant rate or whether factors such as curves or the distance between dominoes affect the speed of the reaction.

If you have not yet done the activity "WAVES ARE MOTION THROUGH A MEDIUM" (in **Part 1: Water**), this would be a good time to introduce the related concept of wave motion. Remind the children that many waves—such as radio and television waves—are invisible to our eyes.

DESCRIBING MOTION DEPENDS ON WHERE YOU ARE

Materials and Supplies
globe

Children often have difficulty understanding that descriptions of motion are relative. Start by talking about left and right in reference to hands and feet. Then divide the class in half with two lines facing each other. Stand at the end of one line and ask the children in that line to tell you which side of them you're on. Move across to the other line and ask the same question. As one line answers "left" and the other "right," it becomes clearer that the starting reference point is crucial to giving direction by left or right.

Use a clock to discuss the concepts of clockwise and counterclockwise. Then stand between the two lines facing each other. While facing one group with your back to the other, rotate your arm in sweeping up-and-down circles. Ask the two lines which direction your arm is turning. The children will understand that the answer depends upon the line they happen to be in.

Now ask: In which direction does the Earth spin? Use a globe to show that the answer depends on whether you look from above the North Pole or from above the South Pole. Establish that the poles are reference points for the directions east, west, north and south. The four compass directions do not change, except for the peculiar instance of someone standing exactly at one of the poles. A person at the south pole, for example, can travel in only one direction, north. Up and down are defined in reference to the Earth: Up is away from the center of the planet; down is toward its center.

Our knowledge of motion and of our position in the universe have undergone great changes over the last several hundred years. Children enjoy learning about the theories people have held throughout history. Fill the science table with books about famous scientists and their important discoveries.

MAKING A BALANCE FOR WEIGHING THINGS

Materials and Supplies
straight piece of wood (dowel, yardstick, or meter stick, etc.)
sturdy string
two of the same type of aluminum pie pans
hammer and nail
thumb tacks

Because it develops comparing skills, balance (or equilibrium) is an important concept for children to learn. They can use the simple balance described in this activity for many weighing experiments as well as for independent exploration.

Start by using a hammer and nail to poke three or four holes around the rims of the pie pans. Cut pieces of string to the same length. Loop the end of one string through the holes in a pan, and then gather the free ends and tie them into a knot. Do the same thing with the other string and pan. Your weighing pans are now ready for use.

The balance must be suspended from above. Tie another piece of string around the center of the long stick, and hang the string from a bracket or similar protrusion from the wall. If you don't have access to a wall mounting, you can attach the balance to another stick suspended between tables or chairs.

Loop the strings attached to the weighing pans over the stick and adjust until the pans balance. Then secure the pans in place by fastening the strings to the stick with thumb tacks. Check your balance by weighing similar objects before moving on to objects of different weights. To find the heavier of two objects, see which pan is lower. If you have objects of known weight, you can use them to balance objects whose weight you are trying to discover

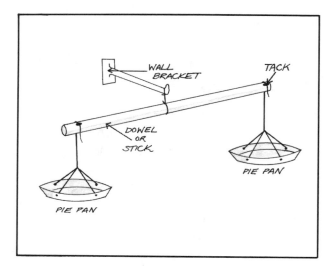

SOUND

After studying waves in the water and motion units, children should be able to visualize how sound travels in wave patterns through air. Since music is probably the most pleasant application of the concept, it offers a good starting point.

HOW DOES A GUITAR WORK?

> *Materials and Supplies*
> hollow box (shoe or cigar box)
> rubber bands
> glue
> pieces of strong cardboard
> wood and nails (optional)
> tuning fork or coat hanger
> water

You can make an entertaining instrument with a hollow box and rubber bands. Circle the box with bands of differing thickness, pluck each one, and have the children compare the tones. Use a tuning fork or a straightened wire coat hanger to demonstrate vibration. Sticking the tuning fork or hanger in water will cause a wave pattern, simulating the sound waves of the rubber bands.

To show how shortening and lengthening the rubber bands affects their pitch, have the children work in pairs with one child stretching a rubber band between his hands while the partner plucks it. After some careful listening, the children should be able to predict the result of lengthening or shortening the band. To make frets, fold rigid cardboard pieces into box shapes and glue them inside the instrument to the bottom. By pressing the rubber band to a fret with your finger, you shorten the rubber band, altering its pitch.

You can make a more permanent guitar by tapping pairs of nails into a flat piece of wood, gradually lengthening the distance between the nails, and then stretching a rubber band around each pair. Strum away! Then have the class examine a piano to see how this basic sound principle functions in a familar instrument.

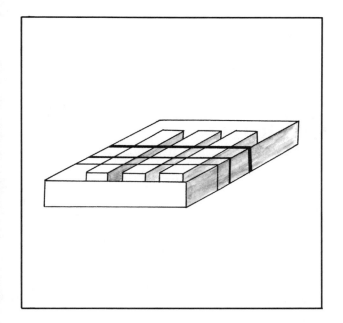

HOW DOES A XYLOPHONE WORK?

Materials and Supplies
set of similar glasses or jars
water
pencils
wooden slats, nails, rope (optional)

Group the children and have them create "xylophones" with glasses or jars containing different amounts of water. Let them experiment by changing the water levels and then determining pitch by tapping the glasses or jars with pencils. Help the children figure out how to raise the pitch: add water or remove it?

If you have access to tools and wood, you can make more sophisticated xylophones. Start by driving nails into the ends of wood slats of different lengths. Then connect the slats with a rope tied around the nails so that the instrument can hang.

SOUND CAN TRAVEL THROUGH THINGS

Materials and Supplies
diverse classroom materials

Children can find it intriguing to discover which materials conduct sound most efficiently. To demonstrate the difference between sound traveling through wood and the air, have a child place her ear to a desk or table top. Then lightly tap the surface of the wood. Have the child lift her head, tap the wood again, and ask her to compare the difference in loudness. You can repeat the demonstration using windows, walls, doors, floors, radiators (make sure they aren't hot!), etc.

Many students know that American Indians used to put their ears to the ground to detect the approach of horses or buffalo. Designate some children to be Indians and others horses before going out to the playground. Let the "Indians" keep their ears to the ground while the "horses" run around, and then switch roles. Ask the children whether pavement and soil are equal conductors of sound.

MAKING A TIN CAN TELEPHONE

> *Materials and Supplies*
> two metal cans with one end cut out
> string
> hammer and nail
> styrofoam or paper cups

This popular activity is too much fun to leave out of any study of sound. Use a hammer and nail to tap a hole through the closed end of one tin can. Knot a string inside the can, and pass the other end out through the hole. Connect the string to the other can in the same manner. When held taut, the string is capable of transmitting whispers across the room. Try making a telephone with styrofoam or paper cups, and compare the results with the tin cans.

MAKING A RECORD PLAYER

> *Materials and Supplies*
> pin or sewing needle
> sheet of paper
> record turntable
> nonvaluable record

Most children think of a record player as a magical device, and they will appreciate it even more after this activity. Pass around a record so that everyone can examine its grooves—under a viewing lens, if possible.

To make a tone arm, roll a piece of paper into a cone shape and insert a pin through the narrow end. Place the record on the turntable, hold the pin to the record, and turn or spin the turntable. The needle will vibrate, and the cone will amplify the resulting sound. You can enjoy a variety of sounds by varying the speed of the turntable.

Let the children take turns holding the tone arm. They will understand that the grooves in the record are a track for the needle to follow. Caution them, however, not to try this activity at home because a nonphonographic needle will damage family records.

WHICH IS FASTER, SOUND OR LIGHT?

> *Materials and Supplies*
> sticks

Divide the class into two groups. Starting in one corner of the schoolyard, let one group move gradually further away from the other. Both groups should take turns knocking sticks together—solid sticks, not so long that they will break in two.

After a while, each group will see the other group bang the sticks before they hear the sound. Explain that this is the same effect you see when you watch a baseball game from far away and you see the ball fly off the bat before the sound reaches your ears. Remember, though, that since sound travels about 1,100 feet per second, you will need a long distance between the two groups for this activity to work.

LIGHT AND COLOR

Humans are extremely visual creatures, and many of our actions are responses to what we see. When we see things, we are actually seeing visible waves—called light—reflected from them. By using a few simple tools and techniques, children can enjoy making many interesting discoveries about light.

CHASING RAINBOWS IN YOUR CLASSROOM

Materials and Supplies
prism
water
pane of glass
white sheet of paper
crayons

The sun is our principal source of light. Sunlight usually appears to be white, but by using a prism or a drop of water, we can split light up into its component colors.

Hold up a prism so that sunlight shines on it. The prism will project a spectrum of colors—or "rainbow"—onto the wall or ceiling. Placing a sheet of white paper in the path of the spectrum will enable the children to study it more closely.

Ask the children to list the colors they see, in order across the spectrum, starting with red and ending with violet. The order is red, orange, yellow, green, blue, indigo, and violet. A mnemonic device for remembering the order is the name "ROY G BIV," composed of the initial letters of the colors in the correct order. Because indigo will probably be unfamiliar to

the children, help them find it on a color chart or in a box of crayons.

A drop of water on a pane of glass will also project a rainbow, but you may find it difficult to hold the glass pane at the proper angle to catch the light. In nature, rainbows are caused by water in the air splitting sunlight into the spectrum colors. Waterfalls are often surrounded by rainbows due to their sprays.

Have the children use crayons to draw and color rainbows. With a little encouragement, they'll soon be placing colors in the order of the spectrum.

MAKING A COLOR WHEEL —HOW OUR EYES SEE MOVING COLORS

Materials and Supplies
paper
scissors
drawing compass (or something round to trace)
pencils
rulers
string or rubber bands
crayons

Can our eyes distinguish colors moving at high speeds? Making and spinning color wheels will provide the answer. A spinning color wheel makes pretty patterns and shows which colors stand out most clearly.

Cut out a round disk from white paper, and use a ruler to draw four lines across the disk through its center. Color seven of the resulting wedges with spectrum colors, and leave the eighth wedge white. If you want, you can combine indigo and violet as purple for one wedge, and then color another wedge black.

Place the disk on the point of a pencil and spin it. Watch the colors as the disk travels at different speeds. Note which colors stand out.

To make the spinning more automatic, thread two strings (or a long rubber band) through the hole in the center of the disk. Then rotate the disk by moving your hands in a circular motion while holding the ends of the strings. Now when you pull on the strings the wheel will spin by itself.

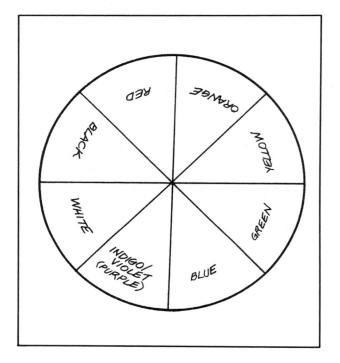

Turn on the flashlight in a darkened room. Gently tap chalk erasers together to produce a cloud of dust in front of the light. The straight path of light will be clearly shown as it reflects off the dust.

While the room is still dark, hold up a book and shine the flashlight at it. Have the children notice the shadow cast behind the book. Clearly, light cannot bend to go behind the book.

Here is another way to demonstrate that light travels in a straight line. Make pencil-point holes in three sheets of paper. Then light a candle and let the children look at the flame through the holes in all three sheets. If one hole is out of line, the light from the candle cannot reach the eyes of the viewer.

WATCHING THE STRAIGHT PATH OF LIGHT

Materials and Supplies
flashlight
chalk erasers
paper
book
candle
pieces of rigid paper
pencil

REFLECTION—BOUNCING LIGHT OFF MIRRORS

Materials and Supplies
flashlight
paper
mirrors
string
balls that bounce easily (e.g., tennis balls, basketballs)

Place a mirror on the floor in a darkened room. As you shine the flashlight on the mirror, have the children note the angle at which the light bounces off it. Hold a book in the path of the reflected light to show the angle at which the light is heading after bouncing off the mirror.

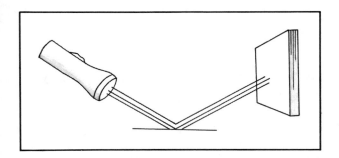

Make the point that the "angle of incidence" (where the light strikes the mirror) is equal to the "angle of reflection" (where the light leaves the mirror). More simply put, the angle "in" equals the angle "out." You can illustrate the point further by using a second mirror to reflect the light again after it bounces off the first mirror.

With the lights back on or outdoors, let the children try to duplicate the "angle in equals angle out" bouncing of light with tennis balls or basketballs. Have the students stand a few feet apart and play catch, tossing one-bounce throws to each other.

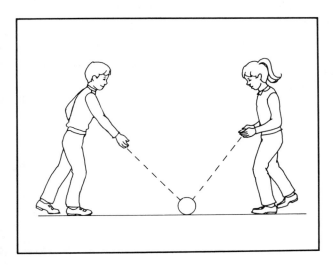

Another way to demonstrate this principle of light reflection is to lay a mirror on the floor in such a way that two children can stand on either side and see each other in it. Tape two pieces of string to the mirror, and let each child hold a string to show the path of light.

To show that we do not see ourselves as others see us when we look in a mirror, hold up a piece of paper with some writing on it in front of a mirror. The writing will appear backwards in the mirror. Then angle two mirrors together as if they were on a hinge. The writing will appear correct. The same is true for a human face looking into a mirror. A single mirror provides a reversed reflection while a hinged mirror allows you to see yourself as others see you.

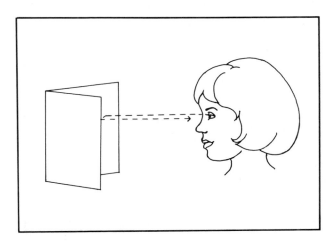

LIGHT TRICKS—FOOLING OUR EYES

Materials and Supplies
postage stamp or sticker
glass of water
book
index cards (or rigid paper
cut to 3×5-inch size)
stapler
straw or dowel

In the section on **Water**, we saw how the refracting or bending of light can fool our eyes. A spoon resting in a glass of water appeared to be broken.

Here's another example of how the effect of water on light can trick us. Place a postage stamp on a table, and set a glass of water on top of the stamp. Cover the top of the water glass with a book. The postage stamp seems to disappear! You can't see it through the sides of the glass because the water bends the light.

Now show the children how our eyes compensate for rapid changes by combining images. Draw a picture on each unlined side of two index cards, and then staple the cards to each other—picture sides out—around a straw or dowel so that they spin easily. Flick the cards with your finger or blow them with a straw to make them spin. Children watching the spinning pictures should see the two drawings appear to merge into one.

MAKING A STROBOSCOPE

Materials and Supplies
cardboard or oaktag
scissors
drawing compass (or round object to trace)
pencil with eraser
thumb tack
ruler

As we saw in the previous activity, our eyes merge images that move too fast for us to see clearly. For example, the rapidly spinning blades of a fan or propeller look like a solid mass. And a projector wheel appears to have no spokes when it speedily rewinds film.

The stroboscope is a tool designed to let the viewer see a moving object at regularly spaced intervals, rather than a continuous view. A simple stroboscope is fun to use because it appears to stop motion.

Cut a large disk—with a diameter of about eight inches—from fairly rigid cardboard or oaktag. Then cut eight narrow, evenly spaced slits in the disk as illustrated below. Attach the disk to the end of a dowel or to the eraser end of a pencil with a thumb tack. Make sure that the disk spins freely.

Spin the stroboscope with your fingers, and have the children look through it at an object that makes a circular motion: e.g., a moving record turntable, open-reel tape recorder, or projector reel. Then let them watch other

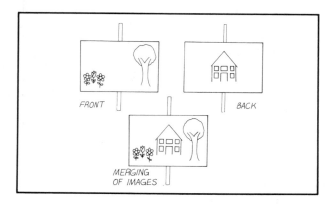

FRONT   BACK

MERGING
OF IMAGES

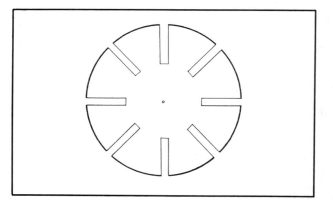

movements—someone running in place, water dripping from a faucet, a yo-yo going up and down, etc. The stroboscope view will resemble a somewhat "jerky" movie. The reason that a motion picture—which is really just a series of still photographs—seems to be continuous movement is that our eyes are used to sustaining images. As images are projected quickly one after the other, our eyes merge them together in one continuous stream.

HOW A LENS WORKS

Materials and Supplies
lens
paper
flashlight
chalk erasers

A lens is a device for bending light. Pass around a reading or magnifying lens so that the children can see how it works as an optical tool.

Then shine a flashlight through the lens and onto a piece of paper held up on the opposite side of the lens. By moving the paper back and forth, you can find the point at which the rays of light converge—or focus. By doing this demonstration in a darkened room and using chalk-dust to outline the path of light, you can show clearly how a lens focuses light.

Ask the children whether moving the flashlight affects the focus (it doesn't). Then ask whether moving the lens affects the focus (it does). Have the children generate a list of uses for lenses, and the next time you prepare to show a movie or film strip, have them pay attention to the focusing mechanism on the projector.

Finally, you can show how the camera was invented, by projecting an image through a lens. Try holding the lens near a window so that it reflects light onto a piece of paper. See if you can make a scene from outdoors appear on the paper.

REFLECTING LIGHT— COMPARING THE COLORS

Materials and Supplies
paint or ink of various colors
white and black paper
flashlight
pieces of colored cellophane

Divide the class into groups, and have each child letter his or her name plainly on a white sheet of paper. Each group should use a different color ink or paint. Go into a darkened room—a large closet works well—and see which names show up most clearly. Use a flashlight to test each color's reflecting power.

An interesting follow-up activity involves using colored cellophane as a filter to color the light of the flashlight. Again, go into a darkened room to see which colors of light from the flashlight seem brightest and which reflect off the colored names on the white sheets of paper. Then repeat the demonstration with a set of names written in white ink or paint on black paper.

Propose to the students that they design a lighting system for night travel. What color should headlights be so that drivers can see the road? What color should taillights be so that cars will be visible to other drivers? What would be a good color to paint road signs or lane markings so that they will be most visible at night? This exercise provides good practice in problem solving.

The opposite of reflecting light is absorbing it. The experiment in **Earth In Space** in which different colors were tested to determine which absorbed the most sunlight and became hottest is a good one to repeat or review at this time. Children should learn that deep, dark colors absorb light while lighter and brighter colors reflect it. Ask them to name the best colors for winter clothing and the best colors for summer clothing. Why do some colors provide warmth while others keep you cool?

SIMPLE MACHINES

Learning how simple machines work can help demystify the world of more complicated machines. Often, the tools and gadgets that surround us are not much more than applications of simple machines.

The term "simple machines" usually includes the inclined plane, wheel and axle, pulley, lever, screw, and wedge. In these activities, the word "ramp" is used instead of "inclined plane" to facilitate understanding.

To augment this unit on simple machines, have your class try to build a small-scale pyramid out of blocks. The children should start by hauling the "stones" (blocks) around the base and then positioning them properly so that the structure grows. Encourage the children to use the simple machines described in this unit to construct their pyramid. This exercise provides good opportunities for problem solving because the children must figure out how to lift the blocks in order to erect a tall building.

when the block is completely off the table. The heavier the object to be lifted, the longer the rubber band becomes, thus demonstrating the amount of energy needed to lift the block.

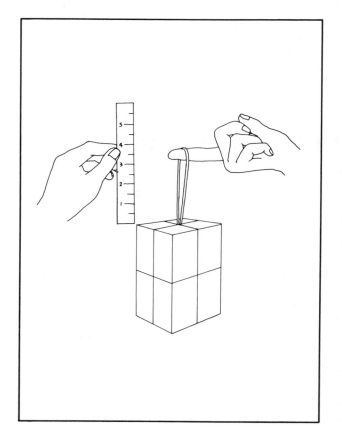

LIFTING THINGS USES ENERGY

Materials and Suppplies
block
rubber band
string
ruler

Loop a string through a rubber band and tie it to a block or other solid, sturdy object. Lift the block by lifting the rubber band, and then measure how long the rubber band becomes

RAMPS MAKE IT EASIER TO LIFT THINGS

Materials and Supplies
block
rubber band
string
ramp (board, large book, or other flat surface propped up at a 45° angle or less)
ruler

Using the same block, rubber band, and string from the previous experiment, drag the block up a ramp by pulling on the rubber band.

Measure the rubber band doing the work. If the rubber band doesn't need to stretch as far as it did in the straight lift, it shows that sliding the block up a ramp requires less energy.

Vary the steepness of the ramp and repeat the demonstration. Record the results at various ramp angles.

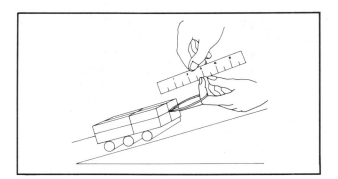

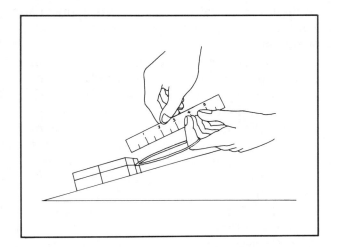

WHEELS—ROLLING SOMETHING IS EASIER THAN DRAGGING

Materials and Supplies
block
rubber band
string
ramp
round pencils or dowels
ruler

Use the same items from the previous demonstrations to pull the block up the ramp, but this time put round pencils or dowels under the block. Measure the length of the rubber band. If it stretches less than before, it shows that wheels (pencils) save work by reducing friction. Rolling something up a ramp requires less energy than sliding it along the surface of the ramp.

A PULLEY CAN HELP DO WORK

Materials and Supplies
block
rubber band
string
pulley or round object (broomstick,
dowel, pointer, etc.)
ruler

To see whether a pulley uses energy more efficiently than a straight lift, tie a foot or two of string to the rubber band, pass the string through the pulley (or over the round stick), and then pull down on the string to lift the block up. Measure the length of the rubber band when the block is off the table.

The rubber band will probably stretch as much as it did on the straight lift, thereby showing no mechanical advantage to a pulley. But that is because a single pulley only serves to change the direction of the energy applied. Pulleys used in combinations (e.g., block and tackle) do reduce the amount of energy needed to lift an object.

The children should come to realize, however, that changing the direction of applied force with a pulley is often very useful. Describe how a pulley can be used with clotheslines to change the direction of the rope. And there are times when a vertical lift of a very heavy object is impossible, but the object can be moved up a ramp with a pulley.

Try to get an actual pulley for this activity. A pulley is inexpensive and fun, and it works much more efficiently than a stick or dowel. If you do use a stick, however, make sure the children who are holding it let it rest between their thumb and index finger and allow it to turn when the string is pulled down over it.

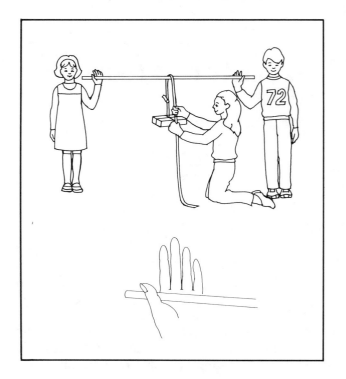

LEVERS—HELPING US MOVE HEAVY OBJECTS

Materials and Supplies
seesaw
broomstick or other long sturdy pole
large rocks

If your playground has a seesaw, you can use it to demonstrate a lever—a device used to lift heavy objects. A lever is a rigid bar supported at a stationary point called a fulcrum. In a seesaw, the fulcrum is the bar under the center of the moving plank.

Children of equal weight, of course, will balance each other when they are at equal distance from the fulcrum. Experiment by moving one child closer to the center. Who gains an advantage? How can a lighter person balance the board when someone heavier is on the other side? Help the children understand that moving away from the fulcrum lengthens that part of the lever, thereby increasing mechanical advantage. Thus, a longer lever can do more work than a shorter one.

Encourage the children to create their own levers outdoors with a broomstick and some rocks, but supervise this activity closely: Kids love to build catapults! Have them start by placing the broomstick under the edge of a heavy rock. Place another rock under the broomstick to use as a fulcrum. Let them try moving the heavy rock while the fulcrum is at several different distances from the object and see if they can detect a difference. They should understand that as the distance increases from A to B in the figure below, the lever can do more work.

See how many common examples of levers the class can list. The crowbar, wheelbarrow, and fishing rod should certainly be on your list.

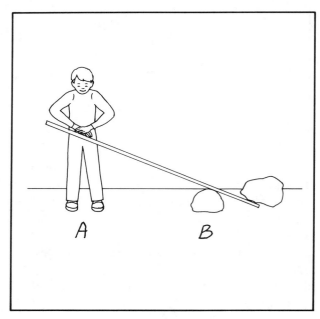

SIMPLE MACHINES AROUND US

> *Materials and Supplies*
> none

Make a list of simple tools in the classroom or school. Your list may turn out to be surprisingly long: stairs (ramp), window sashes (pulleys, levers, screws), book carts (wheels), etc. You might even ask the maintenance staff to demonstrate their tools and to conduct a tour of the heating plant, kitchen, and other places where machines are operating.

Be sure to point out examples of screws and wedges. A screw is a ramp traveling around a cylinder. You can find many examples of wood or metal screws holding materials together or doing work—e.g., doorknobs and pencil sharpeners—in your classroom. Wedges are tools whose surfaces taper to a point or a sharp edge. Knives, axes, and nails are wedges.

Farm machines and engines often capture the imagination of youngsters, and kids enjoy learning about human struggles before advances in technology. Have them try to imagine the work needed to plow a field hundreds of years ago. Make sure your science table includes some books on the development of machines through history.

Remember, too, that school is a valuable recycling center for otherwise useless resources. Always save things that can illustrate how a simple machine functions. A broken watch, for example, can be dissected in class so that the children can examine its gears and springs.

MAGNETISM AND ELECTRICITY

Science often seems like magic to young children. While this science-magic connection is positive in that it encourages kids to approach the natural world with as much wonder and awe as they approach the supernatural world, it also perpetuates the idea that only a small group of specialists can really understand what science is all about.

Experiences with the invisible forces of magnetism and electricity help familiarize children with some basic scientific properties and encourage them to learn more about this fascinating branch of science.

WHAT DOES A MAGNET ATTRACT?

> *Materials and Supplies*
> magnet
> aluminum pie pan
> variety of common objects

Draw a chart with two columns on a large sheet of paper or on the chalkboard. Label one column "Attracts" and the other column "Does not attract." Now try picking up various objects with the magnet, and list each object in the appropriate column. Let the children draw the conclusion that only metal objects are attracted to magnets. Then help them refine that generalization by showing that an aluminum pie plate is not attracted to the magnet. They should understand that not all metals are attracted to magnets. Most commonly, the metal attracted to a magnet is iron or an iron alloy; nickel and cobalt are other metals which magnets attract, but they are less common.

CAN A MAGNET ATTRACT THROUGH DIFFERENT MATERIALS?

Materials and Supplies
magnet
paper clip, thumb tack, or nail
various substances: paper, wood, glass,
cloth, cardboard, etc.

After you establish that a magnet will attract iron and steel (an iron alloy), you can demonstrate that the magnetic field will pass through paper to attract an object.

Put the magnet and a metal object—paper clip, thumb tack, or nail—on opposite sides of a piece of paper to show that the magnetic field passes through the paper. Experiment with papers of different thicknesses. Then see if the magnet can attract through glass (a window pane will work), wood, cloth, cardboard, and other common materials.

If you have iron filings, spread them out a sheet of paper. When you place the magnet under the paper, the filings will outline the magnetic field.

Children enjoy moving a cut-out figure by means of a hidden magnet. Have them tape a paper clip to the figure and then place the figure on a sheet of paper. By moving a magnet be-hind the sheet of paper, they can make the figure perform. In fact, the children can improvise small-scale puppet shows using the hidden magnet method.

FISHING FOR ANSWERS—A GAME WITH MAGNETS

Materials and Supplies
magnets
string
paper clips
glue
index cards or sturdy paper

Here is one entertaining way to practice rote learning with magnets. Write math facts, vocabulary words, or other items of current study on index cards. Glue a paper clip to the back of each card, and place the cards face down on the floor.

Children can then take turns "fishing" for the cards with magnets tied to strings. In order to keep the card "caught," however, the player must correctly answer the math fact problem, read the vocabulary word, etc.

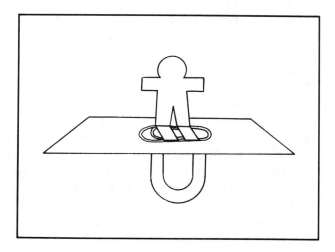

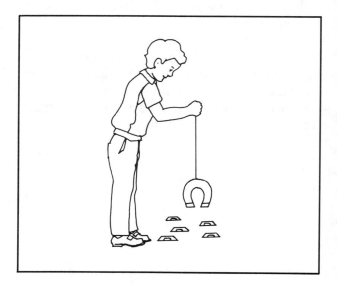

A MAGNET HAS POLES

Materials and Supplies
two bar magnets
string
pencil
books
paper clip

Explain to the children that a magnet, like the planet Earth, has poles. These poles are called north and south because a freely hanging magnet will line up along those directions. Opposite poles attract each other while like poles repel each other.

Tie a string around the middle of a bar magnet and suspend it from a pencil placed across two towers of books. Approach the hanging magnet with a second bar magnet and watch what happens. Does it matter which end of the approaching magnet is closer to the hanging magnet?

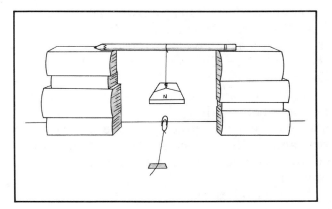

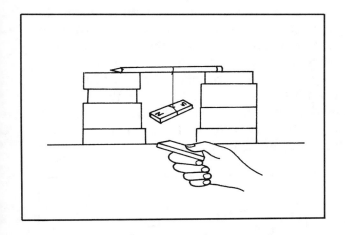

Now tie a paper clip to a string, and approach the hanging magnet with the clip until you feel the pull of the magnet's pole. Find the point at which the clip can be held up by the magnetic field without actually touching the magnet itself. To maintain the clip at this distance from the magnet, attach the string to the table with tape. The paper clip will appear to float in mid-air.

MAKING A MAGNET

Materials and Supplies
magnet
nail or straight pin
paper clips

Children can create their own temporary magnets by repeatedly stroking a nail or straight pin with a magnet. Make sure that they stroke the object in one direction, however, rather than back and forth. Then see how many paper clips the new magnet can attract.

Have the children experiment with different techniques. Does the number of strokes affect the strength of the temporary magnet?

A COMPASS IS A MAGNET

Materials and Supplies
compass
magnet

Refer back to "TELLING DIRECTION BY THE SUN" in the chapter **Earth in Space**, and discuss how we use the sun as a guide to determine direction. The children should recall that the sun "rises" in the southeast and "sets" in the southwest. At mid-day, the sun appears to be in the south.

Demonstrate with the compass that the Earth is really a giant magnet. The compass needle is a much smaller magnet. The Earth attracts the compass needle so that the needle always points to the north.

Now approach the compass needle with a magnet. The children should notice that one side of the magnet attracts one side of the compass and repels the other. This proves that the compass is indeed a magnet. Caution the children, though, that this activity is for demonstration purposes only. Exposure to a magnet can ruin a compass.

ELECTRICAL SAFETY

Materials and Supplies
none

Before embarking upon the following activities involving electricity, be sure to give a short lecture about safety. The children must understand that any electrical experiments have to be done under adult supervision and that the experiments are to be done only with small batteries. They must never fool around with current from the electric company. The electrical current from household outlets is strong enough to injure them seriously.

MAKING AN ELECTROMAGNET

Materials and Supplies
dry cell battery
insulated wire
wire strippers (or pocket knife)
nail
paper clips

It's easy to build an electromagnet to demonstrate the relationship between magnetism and electricity. First discuss how magnetism and electricity work together in electric motors. A magnetic field is created when electrons move along a circuit. Coiling this circuit between the poles of another magnet causes the circuit to rotate and do the work of a motor. The children can compile a list of machines that use electric motors.

Explain that a dry cell battery has a chemical mixture inside which creates electricity—the movement of electrons through metal conductors. By attaching wires to the battery's terminals, we can lead these electrons around a path; this path is called a circuit.

Point out that the insulated wire has copper inside. Copper is a conductor of electricity. For the copper to be part of the circuit, part of the insulation must be stripped away. Use the wire strippers or pocket knife to strip the ends of the wire; older children can use the wire strippers to take off the insulation themselves, but only an adult should use the pocket knife.

Wrap the wire around a nail and connect the stripped wire ends to the battery terminals. Hold the nail near some paper clips and watch what happens: The wrapped nail acts like a magnet. Then disconnect one end of the wire from a battery terminal and see the magnetic field disappear. Explain that it was the electricity traveling around the nail that created the magnet and that the nail lost its magnetism

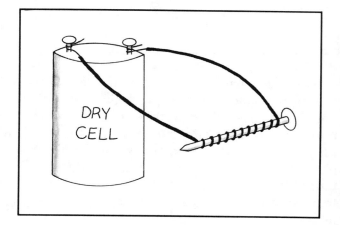

when the circuit was broken, stopping the flow of electricity.

To show that only metal makes successful electromagnets, try wrapping the wire around other kinds of objects: pencils, plastic rods, etc. You can also try to strengthen the magnetic force by increasing the number of loops around the nail and by adding another battery to the circuit. Generally, the more loops and the greater the current or flow of electricity, the greater the electromagnetic force.

MAKING A TELEGRAPH

Materials and Supplies
tin snips
tin can
two boards
two small blocks of wood
hammer
four nails
glue or thumb tacks
dry cell
insulated wire
wire strippers or pocket knife

Before Bell invented the telephone, the telegraph provided a way to transmit messages by electrical signals. You can make a fun, workable telegraph in your classroom with a minimum of materials.

Nail two small blocks of wood to flat pieces of board. Then hammer two nails into each board. Use tin snips to cut two T-shaped pieces out of a flattened tin can. Glue or tack one piece of tin to each small block of wood so that the tin lies above but not on the two nails.

Now wrap wire around the nails and connect one end of the wire to a terminal on the dry cell. Touch the other end of the wire to the second terminal and watch what happens: The nails become electromagnets and draw down the strips of tin with an audible "click." When

you take the wire away from the second terminal, the tin springs back up.

This is basically how the early telegraphs worked. Activating and releasing electromagnets transmitted coded messages via clicking sounds.

To produce a primitive switch for your telegraph (and the next activity), disconnect the wire from the battery and cut it somewhere along the circuit. Reconnect the wire to the battery and then touch and release the cut pieces of wire to turn the telegraph on and off.

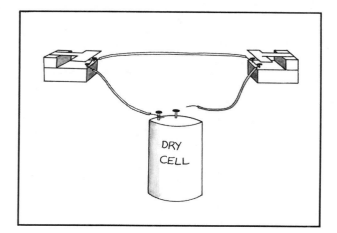

CONDUCTING ELECTRICITY

Materials and Supplies
all materials for the telegraph activity
assortment of ordinary objects (glass, nail, paper tube, cloth, wooden rod, plastic object, rubber object, chalk, coins, etc.)

"Conductors" are materials that electricity can travel through. To find out which materials make good conductors, use the primitive switch from the previous activity—i.e., cut the telegraph wire and strip the ends. Then touch each piece of test material with the ends of the cut wire. Remember to hold the insulated part of the wire. The materials that complete the circuit are good conductors. Have the class make a list of good conductors and poor conductors.

PART 3
Who Lives On Earth?

PLANTS

WHAT PARTS OF PLANTS DO WE EAT?

Materials and Supplies
carrot
celery
lettuce or cabbage
tomato or apple or pepper
mushroom
peas in a pod

As children explore the plant world and the animal world, they can compare and contrast differing life systems. Help them focus their investigation into the varieties of life forms on our planet by asking such questions as: "What do plants and animals need to stay alive?" and "How do plants and animals obtain what they need?"

A clear definition of a plant as opposed to an animal can be elusive due to the difficulty in classifying some small organisms. Let the children suggest attributes for plants and animals, and then let them sort the attributes according to whether they fit both kingdoms or only one. With liberal use of qualifying terms like "most" and "usually" (stay away from "all" and "always"), you probably will end up with a simple working definition like this:

Many plants can produce their own food, and do not move voluntarily. Most animals can move voluntarily, must obtain their food from the environment, and have more complicated systems in their bodies.

You can use this activity as an introductory lesson or on days when you are waiting for other plant activities to yield results. Bring in a variety of fruits and vegetables for the children to eat. Begin by discussing the different parts of plants that we eat. When we eat a carrot, we are eating the root. Celery plants provide stalks to eat, while lettuce and cabbage leaves are the parts we use for food. Tomato, apple, and pepper plants produce edible fruits, while the peas we find growing in pods are actually the seeds of the plant. A mushroom is the entire above-ground portion of a fungus.

Having the children grow a garden offers many wonderful opportunities for plant study. Try to find some protected land near your classroom to cultivate. Plant some early vegetables (radishes, lettuce, spinach) which may mature by the end of the school year, and some very late crops (melons, pumpkins, sunflowers, late corn) which will greet the children when they return in the fall.

This unit deals mostly with green plants. A green plant is one that contains the green matter chlorophyll and can manufacture its own food.

ROOTS

Materials and Supplies
paper cups
potting soil
potato
carrot
turnip
coleus plants
bowls or jars
stones
water

Because the vast majority of plants do not move around to obtain what they need, they must grow parts to perform specific tasks to keep them alive. Roots not only anchor a plant in place but also seek out moisture and nutrients.

ROOTING VEGETABLES. Place the potato in a jar of water, narrow end down. Do not let the water get too high on the potato or it may rot before it develops roots. You can use toothpicks or stones to support it in the jar. You can also use a turnip which will grow roots in the same way.

To grow roots with a carrot, use the freshest carrot you can find and cut off the top two or three inches. Prop up the top part with pebbles in a shallow bowl of water.

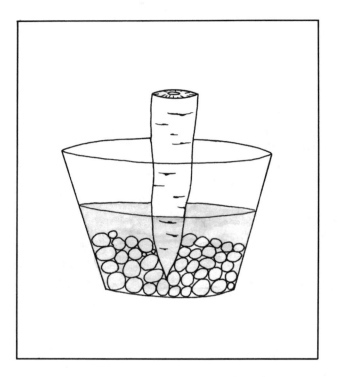

GROWING PLANTS FROM CUTTINGS. Because coleus plants are hardy and easy to grow, they are ideal for use in this unit's activities; start a number of them growing for the class. People who grow coleuses have an abundant supply every September or October for taking cuttings. If necessary, you can substitute nonsucculent house plants—e.g., Swedish ivy, philodendron, begonia, and wax plants—for the coleus, or you can grow these plants in conjunction with the coleus.

Give each child a paper cup, some soil, and a coleus "shoot" or stem. The stem should be about three or four inches tall with several healthy leaves. If you wish, you can have children collect pebbles from outside for drainage in the bottom of the cup. Let them fill their cups with soil to within an inch of the brim. Then have them drill a hole with their fingers down the middle of the soil. They should then place the coleus stem in the hole and gently tamp down the soil around it.

Label each cup with the child's name, place the cups on a tray, and water moderately. At the same time, put a few coleus stems in a jar of water like a bouquet of flowers. When placed in bright but indirect light or in sunlight for a couple of hours daily, the sprouts will grow sturdy and develop new leaves. The stems in the jar of water will soon display white roots, showing the children what is happening beneath the soil in their containers.

During the next two weeks, have the children measure and record the height of their plants each day. Then send the cups home for repotting so that the students will have plants of their own. When kept out of direct sunlight, coleus plants flourish beautifully without much care.

Because sprouting seeds can often be a disappointing activity, be sure to use as wide a variety as possible. Then be patient.

STARTING AN AVOCADO. Although sprouting a new plant from an avocado seed takes a long time (up to two weeks) and is not always successful, the seed is so large that it provides a clear demonstration of how plants with fruits reproduce themselves using well-protected seeds.

Peel the avocado and take the pulp away from the seed. Adventurous students may wish to taste the avocado—especially if you mash it with a little salt. Since you can remove the "skin" around the seed much more easily after it has dried, plan to do this activity over two days or else bring in an avocado seed you have already let dry.

To start your avocado plant, stick three toothpicks into the seed and let it rest pointed side up above a jar filled with water so that the wider end just stays wet. Put the jar in a darkened spot—a closet or the back of a shelf—and check every couple of days. Replenish the water as needed, and change it occasionally.

SEEDS

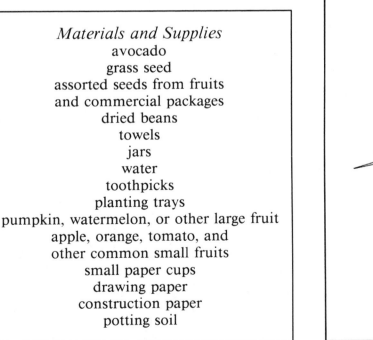

Materials and Supplies
avocado
grass seed
assorted seeds from fruits
and commercial packages
dried beans
towels
jars
water
toothpicks
planting trays
pumpkin, watermelon, or other large fruit
apple, orange, tomato, and
other common small fruits
small paper cups
drawing paper
construction paper
potting soil

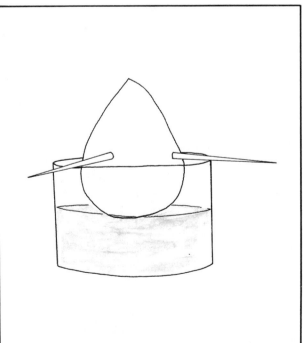

PLANTING FRUIT SEEDS. Children enjoy planting a variety of fruit seeds or pits and then seeing what will grow. Orange, lemon, and grapefruit seeds sprout well.

To simulate the plants' dormant winter phase, experiment with refrigerating some seeds overnight. Some seeds do well when soaked before planting, but others do not. Soaking can speed up the eruption of the baby plant through the seed case.

SPELLING WITH GRASS. Grass seed, if kept damp, sprouts in several days. It will also grow on a moistened sponge.

Let the children use grass seed to create original patterns or to spell their names on potting soil. The grass will grow in the desired shapes.

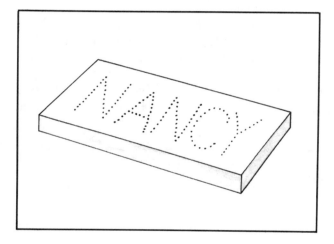

SPROUTING DRIED BEANS. Dried beans—lentils, chickpeas, mung beans, and soy beans among others—are an inexpensive source of seeds for sprouting. To get them to sprout, just roll a paper towel inside a jar and drop the beans between the towel and the glass. Keep the towel moist and the seeds will sprout in a matter of days. You can speed up the sprouting by soaking the seeds for about eight hours before dropping them into the jar.

Inexpensive seeds like dried beans allow you to demonstrate the scientific method. Try sprouting some seeds in a dark desk drawer while you sprout others on a sunny counter top.

Presoak some beans but not others. Put a few other beans in the refrigerator. Then let the children decide what other variables to test, and let them predict what will happen. Explain that this process of experimentation is called the scientific method.

For it to be successful, the scientific method requires careful record keeping. Have the children set up a chart like the one below to keep track of the results of their various experiments.

Bean Sprout Experiments

Jar No.	Presoaked	Location for sprouting	When bean sprouted
1	yes	drawer	
2	no	drawer	
3	yes	counter	
4	no	counter	
5	yes	refrigerator	
6	no	refrigerator	
7	yes	above hot radiator	
8	no	above hot radiator	

COUNTING SEEDS. It takes only one seed to produce a new plant, but not all seeds germinate, or sprout. The germination rates of plants vary, but nature increases the chance for success by producing many seeds per plant. Here is an activity that is perfect for Halloween pumpkin carving. Open a pumpkin (or other large squash or melon) with your class and count the seeds. To avoid losing count midway, use paper cups to store groups of 10 or 50 seeds. Save some of the seeds for "EXPERIMENTING WITH TYPES OF SOIL" later in this unit. If pumpkins are not available, you'll find that many varieties of squash are inexpensive and have large seeds. For a treat, you can roast and eat the seeds.

KEEPING A NATURE SKETCHBOOK. Make a sketchbook for each child by stapling some plain paper between two sheets of construction paper. Have the children decorate the cover and put a title on their sketchbooks. As you study different parts of plants, either out in the field or in the classroom, the children can use their books for sketching specimens. The sketchbooks will keep their work together and maintain a record of their observations.

STEMS

Materials and Supplies
potato
onion
celery stalks
water
jars
food coloring
potting soil or packaged top soil

Although plants do not have hearts, they still move fluid from one area to another. Tree sap is one common example of a moving fluid in a plant.

The intermediaries in this process are stems and stalks. They are what link the water-collecting roots and the food- producing leaves.

SPROUTING VEGETABLES. Two plants whose roots readily sprout stems are potatoes and onions. Children may have seen aging potatoes or onions begin to sprout at home, and you may already have a potato sprouting in your classroom from the roots experiments.

To start a potato or onion sprouting, place the vegetable in a jar of water so that only its bottom end stays wet. The process will soon begin.

POTATOES HAVE EYES. The "eyes" of a potato are actually the buds of new stems. Try burying pieces of a potato with eyes three to four inches deep in the ground outside or in indoor pots. If a large number of children are involved and you must use a number of indoor pots, you can use the coarser and cheaper packaged topsoil available at garden centers instead of the more expensive potting soil. Within a week to ten days, potato stems should emerge through the soil.

COLORING CELERY. This activity is a good one for children who want to see plants in action. Mix some food coloring in water and pour it into jars. Then stand some celery stalks on their bases in the jars, and watch the celery gradually turn color as the colored water makes its way up the stalks.

As a variation on this activity, try splitting a celery stalk and immersing the two halves in separate jars, each jar containing a different food coloring. Watch how the colors progress up the stalks.

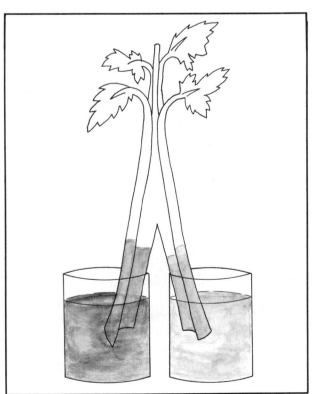

COUNTING TREE RINGS. Tree trunks are actually giant stems. As new cells form each year, the trunk grows wider. When a tree is sawed down, you can see clear lines on the stump marking the divisions between each year's new growth. By counting these annual rings, you can determine how old the tree was when it was felled.

Look around your school yard for stumps to study, and collect large branches that have fallen from trees. Large branches, like stumps, have rings that reveal their age.

LEAVES

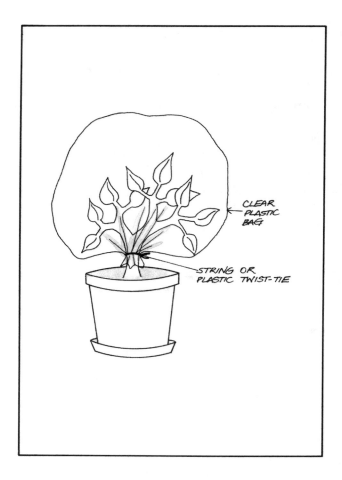

CLEAR PLASTIC BAG

STRING OR PLASTIC TWIST-TIE

Materials and Supplies
indoor plants with leaves
plastic sandwich bags with ties
crayons
paper
leaves and branches from trees
or outdoor plants

It is in their leaves that green plants produce food for living and growing. The process by which leaves absorb light energy from the sun and combine water with minerals and carbon dioxide to make food is called photosynthesis.

TRANSPIRATION. This activity demonstrates the process called transpiration—i.e., a plant emits water vapor. Wrap an air-tight plastic bag around a plant and tie the bag to a stem. Water droplets will appear on the inside of the bag, showing that chemical processes are taking place in the leaves.

Tell the children that plants also give off oxygen, an essential gas for breathing, and help to maintain our atmospheric balance. The carbon dioxide we breathe out is used by plants in photosynthesis.

OBSERVING LEAVES AROUND US. Many leaf activities are dependent on the season. In autumn, have the children watch several kinds of trees and note what colors their leaves turn and when they turn from green to other colors.

In early spring, cut some budding branches and put them in water indoors. A few carefully chosen specimens are all that are needed for sketching and studying with magnifying lenses. Help the children avoid careless overcollecting in the field. Once they become familiar with watching buds emerge indoors, students learn to observe more carefully outdoors as well.

In late spring or summer, have the children lie down under trees and note how leaves grow in patterns to absorb the maximum amount of sunlight.

MAKING LEAF PICTURES. Making leaf pictures is a fun activity for spring, summer, or fall. Arrange the collected leaves on newspaper or scrap paper and cover with a sheet of light or medium weight paper (typewriter or mimeograph paper works well). Rub a crayon over the top sheet and a nice picture of the leaves—showing veins, stems, and edges—will appear.

After they become adept at making leaf rubbings, the children can arrange the leaves into a pattern, or they can work cooperatively to make "trees" on mural paper. To complete the picture with realistic trunks, have them make rubbings of tree bark.

	Water	Sunlight	Results
Plant A	yes	yes	
Plant B	yes	no	
Plant C	no	yes	
Plant D	no	no	

The variables are water and sunlight, and the control is Plant A.

Coleus plants are well suited to this activity because they are extremely resilient. When everyone agrees that a dry plant is dying, water will usually perk up a coleus plant and quickly restore it to health. If plants actually die during the experiment, you could use the event to start a discussion about science needing to sacrifice lives.

WHAT DO PLANTS NEED TO GROW?

Materials and Supplies
four nonsucculent plants
a dark place (closet, etc.)
water

This activity gives the children another chance to use the scientific method. Guide students to speculate as to whether any plant in your classroom can live without water and/or light. Avoid using cactus plants or other succulents in this activity because they can tolerate long periods of drought. Ask how an experiment could determine a plant's needs. Someone should come up with the idea of depriving plants of water and/or light and watching the results.

A chart like the one below will help eliminate confusion about "and/or" while also demonstrating how a "control" and "variables" work.

PLANTS GROW TOWARD THE LIGHT

Materials and Supplies
plants
cardboard boxes
two sponges
string
dried beans
glass jars
paper towels

Examine classroom plants with your students. Help them discover that the leaves face toward the window. Then do the following three activities which demonstrate the phenomenon called heliotropism—plants seeking light.

PLANTS IN BOXES. Place growing plants or sprouted beans in covered cardboard boxes. You can use potted plants or hydroponic (growing in water) cuttings and sprouts. Cut one hole in each box, but make sure that the hole is in a different position in each box.

After two or three days, it will be obvious that the plants are bending and growing toward the holes because that is where the light is coming in.

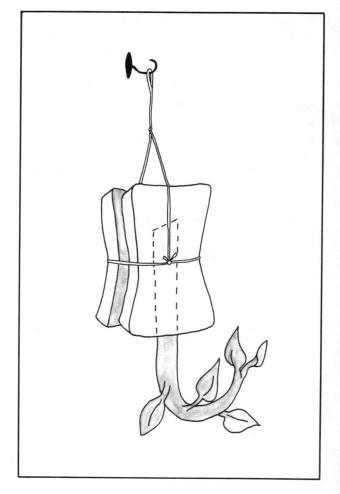

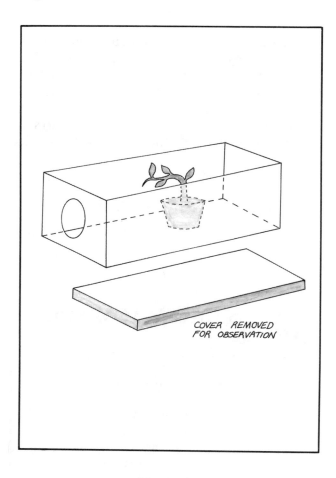

COVER REMOVED
FOR OBSERVATION

UPSIDE-DOWN PLANT. Turning a plant upside down will result in its tip growing in a loop and heading up again. Take a cutting with roots or clip off a healthy stem. Surround the base of the plant by tying two sponges around it. Hang the stem upside down near a window, and keep the sponges damp. Watch the tip of the plant grow back up toward the light.

HELTER-SKELTER SEEDS. In this third activity about heliotropism, repeat the bean-sprouting procedure done earlier in this unit. This time, however, deliberately orient the seeds in all different directions. Place some on their "sides," "backs," upside down, etc.

Then watch how the young sprouts reorient themselves to grow upward. By turning the jar onto a different side each day, you can see how fast the beans change direction.

PLANTS HELP CONTROL EROSION—MARKING A NATURE TRAIL

> *Materials and Supplies*
> scrap wood
> paint

Because their roots bind soil and prevent erosion, plants are vitally important in battling against the loss of topsoil. The activity about erosion in the **Dirt and Rocks** unit—"EROSION IS THE WASHING AWAY OF SOIL"— is recommended for use here in studying plants. To reinforce the concept, take the class on a tour of the local environment to find examples of erosion. Topsoil loss is an acute problem throughout the world, and it certainly deserves attention.

By alerting children to environmental problems, you help prepare them to be conscientious citizens. Ask them why we should stay on paths when we cross through woods and parks. They may well know the answer: When we avoid cutting across areas where plants grow, we allow the plants to take root, hold the soil in place, and provide visually pleasing growth that we all can enjoy. Unlike minerals and fossil fuels, plants are a renewable resource. If we take care of them, they will continue to benefit us.

If you have access to some woods, marking a nature trail can be a very worth while activity. Kids gain an appreciation for the interconnected aspects of nature, and they tend to "adopt" an area and care for it.

Use scrap wood and paint to make simple signs the children can place near interesting points along the trail. Try to have the signs blend in with the habitat, with numbers referring to trees that the children can identify, interesting rock formations, concentrations of particular plants, or other noteworthy features.

The class can produce an accompanying mimeographed booklet for parents, other classes, and visitors. Trail guides you acquired during vacation travels can serve as models and resource material for the class booklet.

WHAT KIND OF SOIL IS BEST?

> *Materials and Supplies*
> coleus shoots
> variety of garden seeds
> potting containers (cups, pots, cans, etc.)
> trowels
> water
> different types of soil
> sand
> magnifying lenses

Plants are almost everywhere. They exist and thrive under a remarkable variety of conditions. Even deserts and arctic areas—landscapes which at some times are too bleak to harbor any life at all—support many species of plants during certain seasons of the year.

Have the children try to think of the most inhospitable environments they can imagine. Then look in encyclopedias or science books to find out which plants live there. Antarctica, for example, is surrounded with an ocean rich in microscopic plants, and in summer the melt-water ponds harbor brief but abundant plant life. In the most extreme conditions, however, where temperatures never break freezing (0° C. or 32° F.), plant life is unable to gain a "toehold." And in desert areas the lack of water is a prime limiting factor for plants.

Remember that green plants, the ones with which we are most familiar, are highly specialized. They require an environment different from one in which plants that do not produce their own food can thrive. For example, there are types of bacteria and fungus that do not require light; these types of plants can even live inside caves.

Each plant grows best in a specific kind of soil. Soil is the accumulation of broken rocks and decaying organic material (humus). Sand contains little if any humus, while soil from the forest floor has few rocks in its upper layers. Commercial potting soil, which is rich in humus, is often sterilized (heated) to kill living organisms.

EXPERIMENTING WITH TYPES OF SOIL. Collect a variety of soils to use for planting coleus shoots and garden seeds. Have some potting soil, dirt from the forest or woods, hard-caked dirt which is not under cultivation, garden soil, and any other type to which you have access. Include some sand in your collection, but not the type packaged for melting winter ice; that type is mixed with salt.

Spread out the soils on newspaper and examine each one with magnifying lenses. List the attributes of each type on a chart. Allow the children to use their own vocabulary: e.g., "hard-packed," "pebbly," "black," etc. Encouraging them to come up with as many characteristics as possible will help improve their powers of observation.

Then plant seeds and sprouts of the same varieties in each type of soil, and place all the containers on the same counter top or table. Have the children observe carefully. Which shoots grow fastest and strongest? In which medium do seeds seem to emerge most quickly? Which soil characteristics from the chart seem to influence plant growth?

Potting soil is the best medium for seeds and

young shoots because it is loosely packed and fairly free of disease, parasites, and competing plants. Hard-packed soil will impede root development. Woods plants like acidic soil and thrive on high concentrations of fresh humus, while cactus plants like sand and often find moisture-retaining potting soil too damp.

If the children enjoy repotting, you can let them transplant some of the woods plants you found when collecting soil samples. Just make sure you don't take any endangered plants, and watch out for poison ivy!

SOIL ANALYSIS. Older or more advanced students will enjoy this supplementary activity. Have them submit their soil samples to an agricultural agency for analysis. Most counties and other jurisdictions offer this service to gardeners and farmers at little or no cost. When they get the results, the children can compare the pH (acidity-alkalinity) readings of soil from different areas.

FUNGI—PLANTS WITHOUT CHLOROPHYLL

Materials and Supplies
wild mushrooms
colored construction paper
glass jars with lids
pieces of bread and fruit
magnifying lenses

A mushroom is a fungus. It has no chlorophyll, which means that it cannot perform photosynthesis to use the sun's energy for the production of food. Fungi grow either as parasites or in conjunction with other plants; in lichen, for example, the partner is algae.

When collecting mushrooms, notice where they grow: in cool, damp areas rich in plant matter. Mushrooms, like other fungi, help perform the important task of breaking down dead plant material, thereby enriching the soil.

MAKING MUSHROOM PICTURES. Start this activity by emphasizing very clearly that the mushrooms gathered for this experiment are not to be eaten. Some mushrooms are deadly poisonous, and there is no easy way to identify the toxic species. If you cannot trust the children to keep things out of their mouths, do not bring them mushroom collecting.

When you have the mushrooms, carefully remove the cap from the stem and look on the underside. Use lenses to study the "gills" or grooves there, and have the children make sketches. Then place the caps on sheets of different colored construction paper, and cover the fungi with inverted glass jars. Leave the jars undisturbed overnight and check the next day.

Mushrooms reproduce by releasing spores from their gills, and evidence of this process should be visible on the construction paper. Spores are somewhat like seeds, but they are more primitive. Spores generally lack the thick protective coating found on seeds, and, consequently, they cannot survive as long as seeds or under as extreme conditions. If you live near a forest, you can find another example of spores by looking under the leaves of ferns.

GROWING FUNGI. Children can grow their own fungi by placing bread or fruit in a jar, putting the lid on the jar, and observing as plants (mold) grow on the food. Have them use magnifying lenses to try to see the spore cases. After watching the fungi for a few days, discard the tightly covered specimens. Reinforce once again that many fungi are unhealthful, although some are deliberately cultivated because they have important commercial and medical uses. Yeasts and antibiotics, along with mushrooms, are examples of fungi in this latter category.

Microscopic mold spores are always present in the air and ready to grow when they find their required conditions—organic material, moisture, and warmth. That is why we refrigerate fresh foods and that is why manufacturers of preserved foods use air-tight canning and chemical mold inhibitors to keep their products safe for human consumption.

ANIMALS

One of the primary goals of elementary science instruction should be teaching children to observe carefully. Once kids begin to look carefully at insects, spiders, and other living things, many of them will be "hooked" on learning more about the variety of fascinating animals around us.

SETTING UP AN ANT FARM

Materials and Supplies
trowel
large glass container (e.g., fish tank or bowl)
fine screening for cover
dark cloth to cover tank
magnifying lenses
access to ant habitat
shoeboxes with top

Ants are remarkable creatures. They live in highly organized colonies and often communicate with each other by rubbing antennae. If possible, show the children close-up photos or images taken by an electron-scanning microscope. Ants have a striking physical appearance, at least as exciting as any science-fiction creature.

Because they are so common and very hardy, ants make a good starting point for an investigation of animal life. Find a place where these busy insects are living (sometimes a piece of rotting wood contains a colony of ants), and scoop them up into a container. An aquarium might be too heavy to carry back to the classroom when full. Consider using shoeboxes to transport ants and dirt.

Look at a book about insects or an encyclopedia to see what the queen looks like, and try to find her when you collect the ant colony. Back in the classroom, fill the tank with dirt—leaving at least two or three inches of space at the top—and gently shake in any ants which remain in the shoeboxes. Set a date for returning the ants back to their original habitat.

This is a closed system; that is, it is not replenished naturally as it would be outdoors. For food, you will need to sprinkle sugar water over the dirt occasionally and add bits of fruit and meat or insects. Cover the container with cloth to keep it dark at all times except when students are observing it, and try to minimize tank movement and disturbance by establishing regular viewing times. If left relatively undisturbed, the ants will tunnel up to the glass.

Use magnifying lenses to watch the ants carefully as they build and maintain a network of tunnels. Be sure to display all the resource books about ants that you can gather. You might want to read *The Grasshopper and the Ant* fable at this time.

DIGGING FOR EARTHWORMS

Materials and Supplies
garden shovels and trowels
string
aluminum foil
planting tray
magnifying lenses
access to earthworm habitat

Some children, especially those who are unfamiliar with gardening, find worms disgusting. Often these kids have never taken a close look at garden soil and the animals inhabiting it.

Although some kinds of worms—such as leeches and pinworms—are harmful to humans, the earthworm is a very beneficial animal. Earthworms help break down the humus, or organic matter, in soil. They eat dead plant material and keep soil loose by crawling through it. Worms breathe through their skin—they must come to the surface when water saturates the soil and forces out the air between particles of earth.

Find an area you can dig up. Divide the class into groups, and assign each group a square measuring about two meters on each side by laying a string or yarn outline on the ground. Let each group member take turns digging and hunting; they are bound to collect some earthworms along with other interesting creatures. Be sure to alert the students in advance to wear work clothes to school on the day of the digging.

Have the children measure the worms they find. Fill a planting tray with soil, and place a few worms in the tray with some old leaves and other decaying plant material. Tear the leaves into tiny pieces. Cover the tray with aluminum foil, and use a pin to punch holes through the foil.

Check the worms and the plant material every two or three days. Have the worms begun to eat the plants? Notice how active the worms have been. Are they grouped together or staying alone? Make sure that the students look closely at the earthworms with magnifying lenses. The children should understand why earthworms are called segmented worms.

At the end of the investigation, release the worms back into the earth where you found them. After having the worms in your classroom for a week or so, you will probably find that even the children who previously disliked worms will act kindly toward these interesting creatures.

HUNTING FOR TINY GAME: COMPARING INSECTS AND SPIDERS

Materials and Supplies
jars with holes punched in their lids
trowels
magnifying lenses

People who don't realize that insects and spiders are members of different classes (under the phylum "*Arthropoda*") often use the names interchangeably. Both insects and spiders have external skeletons, jointed legs, and a segmented body, but there are many differences that distinguish them.

Insects have three body parts—head, thorax, and abdomen— and three pairs of legs. They are the only animals with six legs. Spiders have two body parts—cephalothorax and abdomen—and four pairs of legs.

To find subjects to study, turn over stones, dig into the earth, examine rotting logs, and use a net if you have one. Remind students ahead of time that many insects and spiders bite. One safe method of collection is to place a jar over the insect or spider and slip the punctured top on without touching the prey. Don't put more than one animal in a jar. Because some kids love collecting animals while others find it unpleasant, group the children accordingly to maximize your catch and to encourage peer cooperation.

Bring your catch back to the classroom, and look at them with magnifying lenses. It should soon become clear that insects and spiders are fundamentally different, most obviously in the number of legs—six (insects) and eight (spiders), respectively.

Emphasize to the students that the insects they are observing are adults. Both insects and spiders begin life as eggs. But while spiders—after they hatch—look about the same throughout their lives, many insects pass through three very different stages after hatching. As a larva,

an insect usually resembles a worm and feeds voraciously. Next comes a resting stage in which a pupa develops a hard covering or cocoon. Finally, the adult emerges as the last stage in this metamorphosis. You can watch this exciting change in your classroom. Look outdoors for cocoons to bring in, and when you find some, store each one in a jar with a ventilated top.

By the way, if the kids want to know where "bugs" fit into this picture, tell them that—technically speaking—they are classified as "Hemiptera," an order under the class Insecta. In common use, of course, the term "bugs" refers to many insects.

HOW DO ANIMALS GET AROUND?

Materials and Supplies
mural paper
nature magazines that can be cut up
diagrams of animal tracks

Work with the children to make a chart that lists all the ways in which animals move. As soon as you establish the headings—hopping, swimming crawling, etc.—it will be obvious that a great variety of movement exists in the animal kingdom.

Divide the class into groups, and assign each group one of the chart headings. The groups then can make collages of pictures cut from magazines, each one showing animals traveling in a particular way. Encourage the children to find as wide a range of animals as possible that move in the same way. Of course, some animals move in more than one way, and these animals can appear in more than one collage.

Although hunting through old magazines can be very educational, you can substitute drawing murals for this activity if you do not have magazines available for the children to cut up.

DO THE LOCOMOTION (ANIMAL CHARADES). Through playing charades, or pantomime, children can have fun while thinking about how animals get around. Start by making cards that have the names of familiar animals on them. Then let each player choose a card from a bag and act out the animal's form of locomotion.

ANIMAL TRACKS IN THE CLASS-ROOM. For another activity that encourages the children to simulate animal movement, get a book or poster that shows animal tracks. Copy life-size track patterns onto mural paper, or draw and cut out the paw or hoof prints and lay them on the floor. Then let the children try to follow the tracks.

This activity is best done in small groups because children can find it hard to wait their turn to hop like a rabbit or gallop like a horse. Ask the children if they've ever seen animal tracks in the snow or mud. What animals are likely to make tracks in the schoolyard?

WHERE DO ANIMALS LIVE?

Materials and Supplies
paper
crayons or other drawing tools
photos of animals from different habitats
list of endangered species

Animals are nearly as ubiquitous as plants, but they are harder to find. Help the children compile a list of animals that can be found in the local area, and discuss where each one lives. The class may already have worked with worms, ants, and other creatures that live in the soil and rotting tree parts. And the children will certainly be aware of birds' nests in trees. Discuss the homes of other animals, and be sure to reinforce the importance of leaving wildlife habitats intact. Children must be taught that they must never disturb a nest or hive unless it falls out of a tree and is clearly uninhabited.

Next, expand your list of species to include ones that are not so common. Let the children speculate as to where some of their favorite animals live. Don't be afraid to say, "I don't know," or, "I'm not sure; let's find out." This is the perfect opportunity to motivate kids to read nature books or search out facts in encyclopedias.

After the class has been studying animals for a while, try a sorting activity to help the children place species in their proper habitats. Use photographs of animals from magazines, or collect what you can from colleagues' picture files. Make signs with the names of habitats on them: ocean, woods and forest, plains, polar regions, desert, tropical forest or jungle, and mountain. Have the children paint or crayon a scenic background on each sign and then glue the animal pictures to the appropriate sign— e.g., fish, whale, and sea lion to the ocean sign; deer, squirrel, and bear to the woods and forest sign; rabbit and prairie dog to the plains sign; penguin and polar bear to the polar region sign; scorpion, fox, and snake to the desert sign; monkey and parrot to the tropical forest or jungle sign; and cougar and eagle to the mountain sign.

If you have access to a wide selection of wildlife magazines each year, you can do this activity as a mural rather than as a collection of signs.

DRAWING FOOD CHAINS. A food chain is a series of organisms, each one of which feeds on—and is fed upon by—other organisms in the chain. By studying food chains, your class should begin to understand the interdependence of plants and animals. Interconnected food chains are called food webs.

Begin by tracing the origin of every element in a typical day's lunch. Meat and dairy products come from farm animals raised on grain. Fish are captured from the sea, while fruits and vegetables are grown on farms. Foods in the bread group come from grain grown on farms.

Now have the children construct their own food chains. Plants—which use decaying waste and matter from animals and other plants to produce food—are always at the base of a food chain. Without plants, animals could not survive. Remind the children to include humans (usually at the top) in their food chains.

Here are some food chains to get your students thinking about the interconnectedness of life forms:

    green plants → rabbit → fox
    green plants → moose → wolf
    grass → mouse → weasel → hawk
    plankton → small fish → large
    fish → penguin → seal

When they are finished, the children can illustrate their food chains.

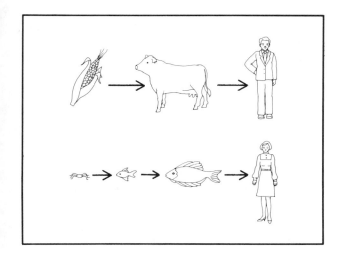

MAKING A FOOD CHAIN CARD GAME.
After the children understand food chains, they will enjoy making and playing this card game. Each card should have the picture of one species of plant or animal from a food chain. Develop the chains in class so that the children are familiar with the relationships among the species. Make the cards from oaktag or other heavy paper, and have the children draw each food chain member and label it.

Each chain is composed of three species. Here are ten food chains as examples:

    corn → cow → human
    plankton → fish → human
    grass → mouse → owl
    grass → mouse → weasel
    fish → penguin → seal
    fly → toad → snake
    water plants → moose → wolf
    green plants → rabbit → fox
    plant matter → worm → robin
    seeds → sparrow → hawk

Two to four children can play at a time. The dealer shuffles and passes out six cards to each player, placing the rest face down in a pile. The player on the dealer's left picks a card from the pile and discards one face up next to the pile. The next player may choose to take either the discarded card or one from the pile. That player then discards a card face up and play continues.

The object of the game is to be the first player with two complete food chains in your hand. If no one wins before the pile of cards is exhausted, shuffle the discard pile, turn it face down, and continue.

THE HUNTER AND THE HUNTED: A PREDATOR/PREY GAME: Explain to the class that a hunting animal is called a predator; a hunted animal is called its prey. Predators use their skills to attempt to capture their prey while animals lower on the food chain try to escape by employing various defenses.

The struggle for survival between predator and prey is one of several factors in nature that control population. When the prey population declines, the environment cannot support so many predators and their population drops too. When that happens, the prey population will increase until the hunting gets easier once again and the predators regain their strength. Thus, the food chain is constantly being balanced by the relative populations of predator and prey.

You can illustrate this balance through a predator-prey tagging game. Establish a rectangular playing area outdoors or inside a gymnasium. Select one-third of the group to be predators; the remaining children in the class are the prey. The predators begin in the middle of the field, with the prey lined up to one side. When you give a signal, the prey try to run from one side of the field to the other.

Prey who are tagged by a predator join the predator team, while prey who escape from one end of the field to the other get to choose an unsuccessful predator (one who didn't catch a prey) for the prey team. If no unsuccessful predators are available, an escaped prey simply lives on to run again.

Outcome Chart

Predator	Prey
Catches prey; prey joins predator team	Captured; joins predator team
Doesn't catch prey; can be chosen for prey team	Escapes predators; chooses a predator to join prey team

Children should come to understand from this game that successful predators will live to reproduce and expand their numbers. Fast, elusive prey will—at the expense of unlucky hunters—also live to reproduce and expand their numbers.

If the whole prey team gets caught and becomes "extinct," the game is over because there is no more food for the predators. In real life, they would have to move on, change their diet, or starve. If the predator population gets wiped out, choose some of the prey to switch teams. In real life, new predators would move in or else the prey would weaken as overpopulation caused their food supply to dwindle.

EXTINCT IS FOREVER. The whole idea of a "natural balance" depends on there being sufficient habitat for predator and prey. Pollution or other means of habitat destruction is a primary cause of some species being put in danger of becoming extinct. Any disruption along the food chain affects all the links, and therefore habitat protection is vital to all life forms.

An endangered species is one whose existence is threatened. Discuss species which are already extinct; dinosaurs, saber- toothed tigers, passenger pigeons, and dodo birds are examples. Acquire a list of currently endangered species by writing to the U.S. Department of the Interior or to various conservation organizations. Once you have the list, have each child in the class choose an endangered species and report to the class about it.

In the early primary classes, children can draw animals in their habitat. Older, more academically advanced kids can research facts about their species and write short essays. Make a bulletin board of student work that will help educate others regarding the plight of threatened animals. And remember, plant species can be endangered, too.

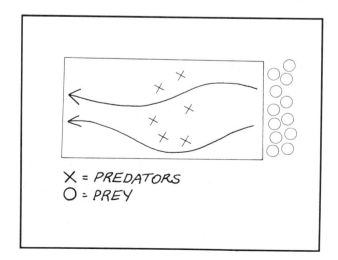

X = PREDATORS
O = PREY

TEACHING TAXONOMY— WRITING BOOKS ABOUT THE ANIMAL KINGDOM

Materials and Supplies
paper
pencils
resource materials about animals

The other activities in this unit have helped demonstrate the vast diversity of animal life. The science of bringing order to this great variety of animals is called taxonomy. Scientists all over the world recognize a two-name system (usually with Greek or Latin names) for identifying species, and while species of plants and animals may be called by many names in many different locations, there is just one internationally recognized scientific name for each species.

Animals are grouped in increasingly narrow categories—from broadest to most specific—according to their attributes. These categories are kingdom, phylum, class, order, family, genus, and species.

Help the children make informative books about taxonomy. Use books, encyclopedias, posters, and other resources for information and illustrations. Younger children in the primary grades can copy text from a chalkboard; older students can write about animals in their own words. In creating their books, the children can practice penmanship and drawing skills.

To begin your discussion of taxonomy, go over the descriptions below in class, covering only one or two a day. Note that phylum names are italicized.

Protozoa: These one-celled animals live in water, soil, and other animals' bodies. You need a microscope to see them.

Porifera: This group consists of sponges. Sponges live in water, grow in many shapes and sizes, and are attached to the bottom; they do not move about.

Worms: Thirteen separate phyla contain worm-like creatures. Some live on land, some live in soil, and some live inside other animals, but they share a common attribute—they do not have a backbone to support their bodies.

Coelenterata: Jellyfish, sea anemones, and coral belong to this phylum. They all have a cavity for digesting food.

Ctenophora: These are the "comb jellies," having hairlike structures on their bodies which propel them through the water.

Entoprocta and Bryozoa: Both of these creatures live in water attached to objects or other living things. They use their tentacles to sweep food into their bodies. *Entoprocta* look like flowers, and *Bryozoa* look like plants.

Brachiopoda and Mollusca: These phyla include such soft-bodied animals as clams, oysters, and snails with protective shells. The octopus and squid also belong to these phyla. They lack a protective shell, but they have strong tentacles and jaws to protect their soft bodies.

Arthropoda: This phylum contains the most animals. Its members all have a segmented body, an external skeleton, and three or more pairs of legs. Insects, spiders, crustaceans (lobsters, crabs, shrimp), centipedes, and millipedes are all arthropods.

Echinodermata: The spiny sea animals—including starfish and sea urchins—belong to this phylum. Most of them have tiny tube feet for moving and eating, and their bodies area arranged like a wheel with appendages going out from a central hub.

Chordata: All of these animals have a rod-like structure which supports the body. Fish, amphibians, reptiles, birds, and mammals are all members of classes with backbones and are known as vertebrates.

Be on the lookout for opportunities for children to observe live animals. In the spring, bring in several large jars of pond water for a week or two and let the students watch the action. Encourage bird feeding at home, and be sure to arrange to have feeders at school restocked during holiday and winter vacation periods.

You can promote nature study all year long in your classroom with indoor activities, but try to take budding scientists "into the field" whenever the weather permits.

THE HUMAN BODY

This unit is designed to provide children with a general understanding of how their bodies are constructed and how they function, along with an appreciation for the complexity of our species. It is by no means a complete course. Many kids and some classes will want to go much more deeply into human anatomy.

Since this unit contains no activities dealing with the reproductive and digestive systems, be prepared to answer questions or to direct children to resources covering these topics. Many children already know a great deal about how pets or livestock or wildlife reproduce and eliminate waste products from their bodies. This unit gives children a chance to understand that humans are animals and that by studying their own bodies they can place themselves as members of the animal kingdom in the natural world.

OUR FIVE SENSES

We are aware of our environment through our senses. Here are some activities to demonstrate the job of each sense. They are just a beginning. Follow the interests you and your class develop, and supplementary activities will grow readily.

SIGHT

Materials and Supplies
cardboard tubes from paper rolls
set of same-sized objects (rulers, pencils, erasers, etc.)

Ask the children to close their eyes and put their hands at their sides. Then, without looking, they should try to touch the tips of their index fingers together in front of them. Make a rule that arms must be kept slightly bent so that no one can simply stretch his arms out full length as a guide. After they try with eyes closed, have the children do the same thing with one eye open. Finally, have them touch their index fingertips together while both eyes are open.

Explain that this activity is easiest to do with both eyes open because our two eyes work together to judge distance, commonly called depth perception. Our eyes can work together because they are on the front of our head. Animals like horses or frogs, whose eyes are on the sides of their heads, cannot judge distance as accurately as humans can.

DEPTH PERCEPTION. Here is another activity that demonstrates how our eyes work together. Divide the class into pairs and give each pair of children two similar objects of the same size. While one child closes her eyes, the other places the two objects on a table or desk at the partner's eye level. The first student opens one eye and tries to guess which object is closer. Have the players take turns, and be sure to vary the viewer-to-object distance.

The difficulty children find in making a choice—as well as the wrong choices they make—will reinforce the importance of two eyes working together for depth perception.

LOOK THROUGH YOUR HAND. To point out another aspect of our "two eyes together" (binocular) vision, try this exciting illusion. Have each child hold a cardboard tube up to one eye and place the other hand directly in front of the other eye. With both eyes open, the youngster will get the distinct sensation of looking through his hand!

This illusion is caused by the fact that both eyes expect to see the same thing from slightly different perspectives. In this case, the brain compensates for the confusion by merging the images. It is this phenomenon that makes us naturally close one eye when we look through a camera or telescope.

Is there a correlation between which eye the children use for viewing through a single opening and right-handedness vs. left-handedness? Usually there is. Count and graph how many children use their right eyes for viewing through the tube and how many use their left. Then do a similar tally of right/left-handedness. Camera makers recognize that most people are right-handed and "right-eyed"; viewers and controls are nearly always on the right—handy for righties but an inconvenience for someone left-handed and "left-eyed."

MORE THINGS TO DO. Use books and posters about optical illusions to illustrate some of the tricks your eyes can play on you. The school nurse or a physician may have informative materials about human sight—e.g., diagrams of the eye, and cards or pictures used to diagnose color blindness. You may also want to refer back to **Light and Color** for additional activities relevant to studying our sense of sight. And helping children discover various art forms around them can make them more aware of how every culture values human sight.

A sobering demonstration you might want to try is intended to make students appreciate their sense of sight. Divide the class into pairs, and then have the students in each pair take turns wearing a blindfold to simulate the loss of sight. A safety lesson about eye care is sure to have great impact following this activity.

room with his eyes closed. Point to another child in the room, and have her clap once. The first player then opens his eyes and tries to guess who made the sound.

Then repeat the game with the guesser covering one ear while his eyes are closed. The kids should discover that it is much harder to judge the direction of noise when using only one ear.

MORE THINGS TO DO. To heighten the children's perception of sounds, ask everyone to be quiet for two minutes. Then have them list all the sounds they heard during that time. Is it ever totally quiet? In almost every environment, silence is a relative term which nearly always includes some low-level background noise.

Music, like visual art, is a universal aspect of human culture. Encourage investigations into different forms of music and the instruments used to produce those musical forms. For example, play a record and have the children identify the instruments they hear. You can also fashion some homemade instruments and have the children copy rhythm patterns from each other.

You may also want to refer back to **Sound** for activities relevant to understanding our sense of hearing. And ask the school health director when the children's hearing will be tested. Try to time your discussion about this vital sense to coincide with the tests.

HEARING

Materials and Supplies
none

You can play a game in class to illustrate how our two ears work together to help us locate the sources of the sounds we hear.

WHERE DID THAT COME FROM? Choose a child to stand in the center of the

SMELL

Materials and Supplies
pieces of cloth
plastic bags with ties
variety of different fragrances
(aftershave, cologne, perfume, vinegar,
onion or garlic juice, etc.)
cardboard squares
tape or white glue

Cut bits of cloth and use them to dip into each of the fragrant liquids. Use tape or white glue to mount each piece of cloth on cardboard, and write the name of the fragrant substance on the back. Then have the children take turns trying to identify the various liquids. Be sure to prepare as wide a variety of fragrances as possible. Ask the children whether they find their sense of smell getting dulled after the first few sniffs.

If you dip two pieces of cloth in the various fragrances, you can have the kids try to match them in pairs. As they do, put one piece in its own plastic bag, closed tightly with a tie, and leave its match out in the air (unless the smell is too distracting in a small classroom!). Have the children check each day by comparing the two. Which seems stronger and which weaker? Smells are carried by airborne molecules, and odors diminish as molecules escape. The specimens enclosed in airtight plastic bags should retain more of their pungency because fewer of their molecules can escape. Animals use their senses—including the sense of smell—to obtain food. Although humans do not hunt by smell like some other animals, we certainly make choices about what we eat based on odors. Make a list of the children's favorite food smells. This list can lead nicely into the next activity.

TASTE

Materials and Supplies
salty water
sugar water
lemon water
water-diluted coffee
four small cups per child or group of children
four sticks per child (coffee stirrers, straws, toothpicks, or popsicle sticks)
one glass of water per child

List the children's favorite foods. How does this list correlate with the list of favorite food smells from the preceding section? Most likely it will be similar if not identical. Foods that smell good usually taste good. We have taste buds on our tongues and palates which can discriminate among four flavor characteristics: sweet, sour, bitter, and salty. Our sense of smell helps us discriminate further. When our nose gets congested due to a cold, therefore, our sense of taste is severely diminished.

Use the four solutions to demonstrate how our taste buds react. Give each child or group of children four cups of liquid, each containing a different solution but marked in code (e.g., A, B, C, D or 1, 2, 3, 4). Have the children dip one of their sticks into one of the solutions (everyone does the same solution simultaneously) and touch the stick to their tongues. Remember to emphasize hygiene; children should not share sticks or dip used ones into each other's solutions.

Discuss the taste and ask the students to locate where in their mouths they sense the flavor. We sense bitter tastes at the back of the tongue and sweet tastes near the tip; sour tastes dominate the sides of the tongue while salty tastes can be sensed fairly evenly throughout the mouth. As a result, bitter medicine must be swallowed quickly so that it rushes, rather than lingers over the taste buds at the back of the mouth. Coffee drinkers enjoy the gulp which sends the rich flavor across the same area, and nearly everyone likes to lick ice cream or lollipops so that the tips of our tongues can savor the sweetness.

Repeat this procedure for each of the four solutions, having the children drink water between tastes. The children should be able to discriminate among the four flavors and recognize where in their mouths the taste is most clearly sensed.

TOUCH

Materials and Supplies
empty cardboard boxes
objects with different tactile attributes
(scratchy, soft, hard, wooden, metallic,
rubber, etc.)
gloves or mittens

The skin over our bodies contains cells which, when stimulated, transmit information to our brains. These cells—nerve endings—are concentrated in areas of our bodies that are the most sensitive to touch. Our lips, for example, are densely populated with nerve endings.

This activity will help students learn that our hands and fingers are sensitive and perceptive guides to the world around us. Divide the class into groups and give each group an empty cardboard box with an opening cut in it. Let the children take turns hiding different objects in the box.

After an object is placed in the box, ask a child who has not seen the thing hidden to roll up her sleeve and reach her arm inside. Can she identify the object by rubbing her forearm against it? Does she find it easier to identify the hidden object with her hand or fingers?

Have the students try feeling similar sized objects inside the box while wearing mittens or gloves. The touch-and-feel game is much harder with mittens or gloves on because players must rely on shape alone rather than shape and texture together.

Discuss the textures that children perceive as pleasant as opposed to those they perceive as unpleasant. It is likely they will use adjectives such as soft, cuddly, and furry in regard to the pleasant textures while terming unpleasant textures gooey, sticky, messy, etc.

SUMMING UP THE SENSES

Materials and Supplies
paper
pencils
art materials for drawing or painting

After studying and discussing each sense with your class, construct a chart that lists the ways we use each sense. Ask the students to name the senses we rely on most. How do we compare with other animals in the use of our senses? Imagine having "super" senses—being able to see like an owl or eagle, hear as well as a bat or dolphin, detect smells like a bloodhound, possess thousands of taste buds like a rabbit, or have the spider's delicate sense of touch! Some students may enjoy comparing the senses of comic book "super heroes" with those of mere mortals.

Humans do not possess particularly proficient senses compared to some of our fellow animals. We do, however, utilize all our capabilities to some degree. Our brains process the information that our senses gather, enabling us to cope well with our environment.

Do humans have more than five senses? Many people claim to have a sixth sense, a feeling that something is happening or will happen but is not perceived by sight, sound, smell, taste, or touch. Another "sixth" sense is the sense of balance. The organs that maintain equilibrium in the human body are located in the inner ear.

OUR HEARTS PUMP BLOOD

Materials and Supplies
watch or clock with a second hand

Our hearts pump the blood that carries materials necessary for our survival to all parts of our body. The pulse we feel is the throbbing of the arteries caused by the heart's contractions.

Helping a child find his pulse can be difficult but very rewarding and meaningful. Try to feel the wrist pulse first. Using one index finger, trace a line down the other index finger to the wrist. Press that spot to feel blood moving through an artery. Do not use a thumb for finding the pulse because it contains a pulse of its own and may cause confusion. Help children who have difficulty finding their wrist pulse by finding the pulse yourself and then directing their fingers to the spot.

Students might find it easier to locate the pulse in their necks. The carotid arteries, which can be felt slightly to either side of the windpipe, present a stronger pulse than the one in the wrist. Another strong pulse is located on the inside of the arm, about halfway between the armpit and elbow.

After everyone has become fairly proficient at finding a pulse, tell the children to count their pulse beats—silently—as you time them for fifteen seconds. If the youngsters must count aloud, encourage them to do so softly, and have only part of the class do the activity at one time. Multiply each student's fifteen-second total by four to determine the heart rate per minute. Record the results.

Next, have everyone run in place for one minute, and then have each student immediately repeat the fifteen-second pulse count. When you record these heart rates, it will become readily apparent that exercise increases the rate at which the heart pumps blood to the body.

You might want to extend this experiment to measure heart rates at different times of the day during various activities. Let everyone lie down and breathe deeply while taking a pulse count to see how slowly their hearts can beat. Check heart rates right after gym or recess for a contrast. How long after exercising does it take for heart rates to return to normal resting rates?

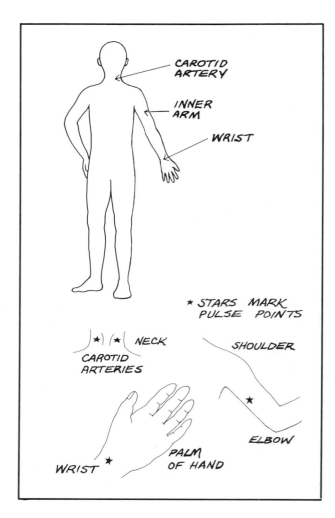

BREATHING

Materials and Supplies
watch or clock with a second hand
balloons

Have the children cup their hands lightly over their noses and mouths while breathing normally. Explain that the air they feel against their palms comes from their lungs. Help them understand how our hearts and lungs work together to supply the body with oxygen and to remove carbon dioxide. As we exercise and expend energy, our breathing rate increases to obtain more oxygen and our heart rate rises to deliver that oxygen to all parts of our bodies.

Have the children count the number of times they breathe in a minute. Younger children might need to keep a tally of their breathing to avoid losing count. Record the results and then have a period of running in place. Count the breathing rates again for one minute and record the numbers.

When were the children breathing the fastest? Our fastest breathing occurs during and immediately after vigorous exercise. We recover to low breathing rates fairly rapidly. You can demonstrate this fact by running in place again, but this time count breaths for just fifteen seconds after stopping. Multiply the count by four to get the minute rate. The children should see that this number is greater than the earlier number, showing that breathing rates slow down rapidly from their peak within the first minute of rest after exercise.

THE BELLOWS. You can use the analogy of a blacksmith's bellows to introduce the children to the way our lungs function. Our lungs, like bellows, expand and collapse with each breath. When we need more energy, we pump the bellows faster to heat up the fire.

Discuss the position and function of the diaphragm, the main muscle of breathing. Just below the sternum (breastbone), the diaphragm "pumps" the lungs which, unlike the heart, do not have muscles themselves for pumping. As we breathe in, the diaphragm rises and our lungs fill, or expand. As we breathe out, the diaphragm relaxes and falls while our lungs empty.

While learning how their lungs work, the children can also work on a valuable relaxation technique. Have them lie on their backs with arms at their sides. Instruct them to take long, slow, quiet breaths. Ask them to imagine that the air they are drawing in through their noses is going all the way down to their bellies, making their navels rise. If you tell them to count breaths, they soon will be slowing down and stretching out each breath, a process that will make them calm. After a few minutes of this relaxation breathing, the entire class should be pretty calm.

"Take a deep breath" is more than a figurative expression for slow down. By slowing down the action of our lungs, or bellows, we can make our entire bodies more relaxed.

HOW BIG ARE OUR LUNGS? Give each child a balloon, and tell the class to inflate and deflate the balloons several times so that they will be easier to fill. Then have each child take a deep breath and inflate the balloon as fully as possible with a single breath. The quantity (volume) of air in the balloon will be approximately equal to the quantity of air that was in each child's lungs.

MUSCLES

Materials and Supplies
hard-covered books
anatomy charts

If you have access to any visual resources that depict the internal workings of the human body, now is a good time to display them. Children are usually fascinated by anatomy charts or posters showing the body's muscles, bones, and organs.

Here's a demonstration that shows what happens to a muscle when it gets tired. Have each child hold a hardcover book straight out to the side at shoulder height. In a little while, their arms will begin to shake and quiver.

It's fun to isolate muscles. While they are holding their books out to the side, have the children feel their shoulder region and try to isolate the area where the muscle has become hard (contracted). This muscle is called the deltoid muscle, and one of its jobs is to lift the arm. Tell the children to put their books down and rest for a while. How does the deltoid muscle feel when it is not contracted?

Here are four other exercises which clearly demonstrate the contracting of a major muscle. During each exercise, ask the children to point to the muscle which becomes hard, or contracted. Explain the difference between flexors—muscles which bend a limb—and extensors which straighten a limb. And caution the children not to try lifting too much weight. Many jobs are too heavy for our bodies, and we can injure ourselves if we try to do something that our muscles cannot handle.

Isometric exercises are designed to make muscles strongly contract even though there is little actual movement involved. You gradually contract the muscles until you feel a slight strain, hold for a few seconds, and then gradually release the tension. Demonstrate how an isometric exercise makes muscles contract without movement by pressing your palms together in front of your chest.

1. Have the children stand beside a table and place four fingers of one hand under its top. Ask them to push up on the table top from below and figure out which muscle is doing the work. See if each student can locate the biceps muscle with the other hand. Now have them place their fingers on top of the table and press down; they should be able to feel the contraction of their triceps muscles at the backs of their arms. The biceps (flexors) and triceps (extensors) present a good example of how muscles work in teams and often in opposite directions.

2. The muscles of the abdomen work to lift the legs. Have everyone lie down and try to lift both legs a few inches off the floor. Caution the children that this is difficult and that they should be careful not to strain their muscles. In fact, they can feel the contraction of their abdominal muscles without their feet actually leaving the floor.

3. People can lift and move a great deal of weight by bending their knees and using their powerful thigh muscles, the body's largest. Children can feel these muscles by lifting the lower leg back and up toward the hip while pressing a hand against the back of the thigh. To feel other thigh muscles contract, the kids should bend their knees and put their hands on the front of their thighs. Contrast these long, powerful muscles with the shorter biceps and

triceps. Which muscle group, arms or legs, would seem more able to lift heavy objects?

4. Finally, have the children stand on their toes and feel the backs of their legs. These calf muscles work hard every day, flexing and lifting our heels off the ground as we walk and run. Now have the children rock back and stand on their heels. They can feel the muscles in the front of their lower legs contract when they lift their toes off the ground.

To reinforce the names of the muscles or their functions, try doing these exercises again, this time pointing to a muscle and asking the children to perform a movement which would cause it to contract. And remember to tell the physical education teacher that your class is studying muscles; he or she could be a valuable teaching partner.

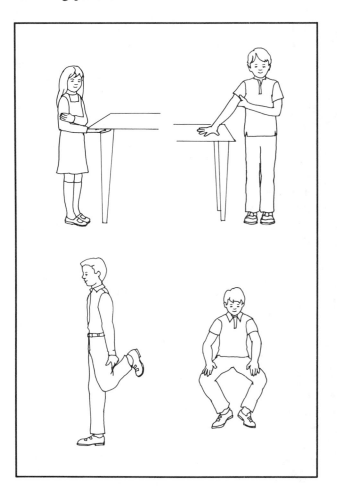

BONES

> *Materials and Supplies*
> scraps of clay, plasticene, or styrofoam
> toothpicks
> resource materials about skeletons

Muscles give our bodies much of their form and shape, but we depend on bones for support. Children can feel the bones in many parts of their bodies: hands, wrists, arms, feet, ankles, legs, heads, collarbones, hips, ribs, knees, and so on. Pictures of bones (especially skeletons!) are always extremely popular, and they are sure to raise interest in the subject and lead to a good discussion.

COMPARING OUR BODIES TO MACHINES. Review the biceps/triceps exercise from the preceding activity, and explain how our muscles usually pull against our skeltons when they contract. When our biceps contracts, which part of the body can lift? Help the children see that the muscle in the upper arm can move the lower arm. What simple machine does this action of the arm bring to mind? Our arms are like levers, and you can compare them to a seesaw, crane, mechanical shovel, back hoe, steam shovel, fishing rod, etc.

Help students discover that bones do not move themselves. Muscles from other parts of the body move them. Abdominal muscles lift the bones in the legs, while leg muscles move the bones in the feet. For a graphic demonstration of the interaction between muscles and bones, have the students feel how the muscles in their necks support and move their heads (skulls).

MAKING SKELETONS. The places where bones come together are called joints. Since bones are rigid, joints are crucial to our being able to move. Any place we want to bend must have a movable joint there.

Have the children connect toothpicks (representing bones) with small balls of clay or styrofoam (representing joints) to make a simpli-fied model of a human skeleton. Make sure the children have plenty of joint material—modeling clay or plasticene works well, especially if you plan to dismantle the skeletons and save the components—and toothpicks. This project enables children to "peek inside," getting an idea of the design of our supporting frame.

The kids can break the toothpicks into different lengths to represent bones of different sizes. Emphasize that they must put a joint wherever the skeleton is to have mobility. Ask them to help you compile a list of joints while they are building their skeletons, and then use that list to contrast the mobility of specific joints: elbow vs. shoulder, knee vs. ankle, etc.

You can hang these homemade skeletons as mobiles or make them stand up by embedding the legs in clay bases. If the project is a success, encourage the children to create skeletons of animals—or even of fantasy creatures!

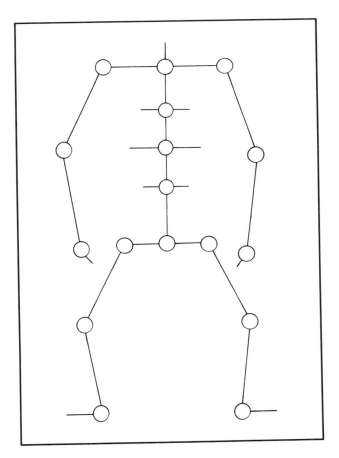

TEETH

Materials and Supplies
mirrors
animal photos showing teeth
apples

Children in the early elementary grades develop a special interest in teeth as their first set begins to fall out and their adult teeth grow in. Take advantage of this natural interest in teeth to teach sound hygiene practices. You can usually obtain information and/or materials from local dentists, some of whom would no doubt enjoy speaking to your class.

COUNTING TEETH. Give a mirror to each child or group of children, and let them count their teeth and record the number. The maximum number of deciduous (milk or baby) teeth is twenty. Tell the kids that as adults they may grow as many as thirty-two teeth.

See how many different kinds of teeth the children can identify. Provide the names as they describe and sketch the various kinds. The eight front teeth are incisors; they make "incisions." The four with the sharp points are canines—"dog teeth." Then come eight pre-molars or bicuspids and, in adults, twelve molars; these teeth are for grinding. Some adults have only eight molars because their "wisdom teeth" never erupt through the gums.

DIFFERENCES AMONG ANIMALS' TEETH. You may be able to tell a lot about what an animal eats by looking closely at its teeth. Because humans eat both plants and animal meat, we need grinding and tearing teeth. See if you can find photographs of sharp-toothed mammals to illustrate the importance of incisors and canine teeth for meat-eating animals.

What kind of teeth do grazing animals need? The flat teeth of ungulates (hoofed animals) provide a good example of the flat, molar-type teeth needed for chewing plants. The children will enjoy trying to guess what various animals might eat by looking at pictures of their teeth.

OUR TEETH AT WORK. To illustrate how human teeth work, pass out apples or apple halves, and tell the children to take one bite. Can they see their teeth marks in what is left of the apple? Emphasize that everyone's teeth are unique; no two sets are exactly alike.

Then have the children take another bite while concentrating on the path that the apple follows through their mouths. Which teeth take a piece off the fruit? Which teeth grind the piece up into bits small enough to swallow and digest?

ARE HUMANS LARGE OR SMALL?

Materials and Supplies
none

Ask this question in class and you will probably find advocates for both positions. Humans are small compared to elephants or blue whales, but they are large compared to squirrels and robins.

Have the children identify animals that are larger and smaller than humans, and record the results on a piece of chart paper. If they suggest general categories of animals (e.g., fish or birds), remind them that those categories contain species of many different sizes.

When you finish the list, you may find that the class has named more larger animals than smaller ones. That is because the large animals are more familiar. In reality, however, species smaller than humans acount for about 99 percent of the animal world. Scientists have discovered and classified more than one million species, and about three-quarters of the total belong to one phylum: *Arthropoda*. In other words, the insects, crabs, spiders, centipedes, shrimp, crayfish, and other arthropods make up more than 75 percent of all the animals known to exist on this planet.